NATURAL RADIANCE

NATURAL RADIANCE

AWAKENING TO YOUR GREAT PERFECTION

LAMA SURYA DAS

SOUNDS TRUE
Boulder, Colorado

Sounds True, Inc., Boulder CO 80306
© 2007 Lama Surya Das ℗ Sounds True

Printed in Canada

ISBN: 978-1-59179-612-1

Other learning programs by Lama Surya Das
available through Sounds True:
Natural Perfection, cassette (1999)
Tibetan Dream Yoga, cassette, CD, or downloadable audio (2000)
Tibetan Energy Yoga, video (2000), DVD (2004)
Natural Meditation, video (2000), DVD (2005)
Buddha Is As Buddha Does, CD, or downloadable audio (2007)

Library of Congress Control Number: 2005924368

As for View, Meditation, Action, and their Fruit:
Make freedom from aversion and attachment your View,
Make destruction of grasping intellectualization your Meditation,
Let freedom from craving and contrived deeds be your Conduct,
Let your Fruit be the abandonment of the wish to attain anything,
And thus realize the Dharmakaya which is spontaneously within!

—DUDJOM RINPOCHE

TABLE OF CONTENTS

INTRODUCTION

Dzogchen is extremely simple, but not easy.

—KHENPO NGAGA

I first traveled to Kathmandu, Nepal, in 1971. My purpose was to find answers to my many questions about the meaning and purpose of human existence. When Lama Thubten Yeshe accepted me as a student, I began to study and practice the 2,500-year-old teachings of Buddhism—in particular, Tibetan Buddhism.

In the years that followed, I had the good fortune to meet and study with some of the great teachers of our time: among them Kalu Rinpoche, Dilgo Khyentse Rinpoche, Deshung Rinpoche, the Sixteenth Gyalwa Karmapa, Nyoshul Khenpo Rinpoche, Tulku Urgyen Rinpoche, Kyabje Dudjom Rinpoche, and His Holiness the Dalai Lama. I also studied with many yogis and Hindu gurus—notably, Neem Karoli Baba (Maharaji), who named me Surya Das (servant of the sun[light]). I spent ten years studying and practicing in the Himalayas, then completed two consecutive cloistered three-year Dzogchen meditation retreats under Khyentse Rinpoche's guidance in France.

During this time, I received a wealth of authentic, life-changing teachings, initiations, and pith instructions from all four major Tibetan lineages. But, ultimately, the teachings that spoke to me most strongly transcended all doctrinal and technical variations. These were the Dzogchen (natural perfection) teachings, which first appeared in India in 200 BCE and migrated to Tibet 900 years later. It is in this tradition that I became a lineage holder, and it is this practice that I mainly teach.

Dzogchen is naked awareness practice, which is to say that it does not depend on images, cultural forms, or outer accoutrements. Dzogchen's unique message is that we are, by nature, all buddhas, for whom enlightenment is possible within this lifetime.

Lama Jamgon Kongtrul Lodro Thaye has said of Dzogchen:

> *It is too close, so we overlook it.*
> *It seems too good to be true, so we cannot believe it.*
> *It is too profound, so we cannot fathom it.*
> *It is not outside ourselves, so we cannot attain it anew.*

Through the practices taught in this program and the guided practices included on the enclosed CD, you will directly experience your own buddha nature and learn that it is available to you in every moment—and that you can awaken to it simply by recognizing how it already exists in your life. Of course, to come to know this underlying truth for ourselves most often takes considerable spiritual study and practice as we travel along the liberating path known as the path of awakening, the great way of freedom and enlightenment.

> *This Is the Time of Dzogchen*
> *This is the moment of Dzogchen, the fourth time—*
> *beyond linear time past present and future—*
> *the timeless time of nowness.*
> *Don't overlook it!*
> —NYOSHUL KHENPO RINPOCHE

Dzogchen is considered to be the summit of all the nine vehicles or approaches of Buddhism. Thus, it is called *Ati* (Peak) *Yoga* or *Ati Yana,* the Peak Vehicle, or *Maha Sandhi,* the Complete Perfection or the Consummate Teaching. Over the centuries, Dzogchen has traditionally been a secret teaching, for initiates only, since this advanced teaching is the direct route to enlightenment, providing immediate access to the ultimate reality, including the totality of innate wakefulness without many steps, studies, purifications, preparations, or gradual practices. Thus, it is known as part of the renowned Shortcut of the Vajrayana (indestructible vehicle), the Tantric path of Buddhism. It has been called "the practice of buddhas, not ordinary beings." When you practice it, you activate and participate in your own buddhaness, right here and now.

Guru Padmasambhava, who brought Buddhism to Tibet in the eighth century, predicted that Dzogchen would be the teaching for a future time when there are dangers in abundance, when people's faculties are keen, and time is short. What better time than now?

In our secular, postmodern age, people of the highest capacities are interested in—and searching for—the final word on enlightenment. These direct teachings of naked awareness and "pointing-out instructions" directly reveal the radiant face of immanent buddhaness and the inherent freedom and perfection of being that is the natural state of enlightenment.

Thus the veil of secrecy has been lifted, and Dzogchen has been taught in several countries by modern masters, including His Holiness the Dalai Lama, Namkhai Norbu, and others, even to people who have not previously studied much Buddhism. My late teacher Tulku Urgyen Rinpoche used to say, "Bring the scientists; they have the sharp capacities to be able to understand these naked teachings." Khenpo Jigme Phuntsok, one of Tibet's greatest lamas, who just recently passed away in eastern Tibet, was famous for saying publicly on many occasions: "This is the time of Dzogchen."

My own teacher and personal mentor, the late Nyoshul Khenpo Rinpoche, used to say, "The Dzogchen view and meditation is in accord with all practices, and is supreme. The view of Dzogchen will enhance any relative practice, Buddhist or otherwise." He told me to be fearless in teaching it to those who seemed ready in the West, and we taught together and led Dzogchen retreats on many occasions. During the 1980s, when he was living in France, he often saw people riding on the Metro in Paris who he thought could be woken up with a single sentence of Dzogchen teaching, if he only had the chance to communicate with them. He taught that Dzogchen's introduction to our naked awareness as the genuine buddha is a teaching for today, a practice stripped of rituals and elaborations, religion, history, philosophy, cosmology, and cultural trappings. It is what the late great

Nyingmapa leader and Dzogchen master and visionary His Holiness Dudjom Rinpoche used to call "the panaceiac wisdom-essence, the single knowing which liberates all."

EMAHO!

"Emaho!" is the shortest Dzogchen teaching. The word means "wondrous," "amazing," "far-out," "fantastic." It expresses the joy and wonder—amazement, really—of discovering within ourselves and our world the radiant splendor of our innate natural state directly perceived by our own eyes, the great completeness, wholeness, and oneness of all that is. As the fourteenth-century Dzogchen master Longchenpa sang, "Since things are perfect and complete just as they are, beyond good and bad, without adopting and rejecting, one just bursts out laughing!" May the Dzogchen meditation practices in this program become a practice path that will deliver you to such joyous freedom and delight. Emaho!

1

THE STORY OF TIBETAN BUDDHISM

꽃|꽃

To abandon what is harmful,
To adopt what is wholesome,
To purify the heart and mind:
This is the teaching of the Buddha.

—GAUTAMA BUDDHA

Buddhism originated with Gautama Buddha (563–483 BCE), a historical figure who was born a prince of Lumbini in northern India—which is now Nepal—and lived for eighty years. He sat and was enlightened beneath the bodhi tree at Bodh Gaya on the banks of the Neranjara River in the wilderness of northern India, 2,500 years ago. But enlightenment and Buddhist wisdom and teachings are not just things from the remote past, when one enlightened buddha walked this earth. Buddhism teaches that we can all become as enlightened, free, compassionate, loving, wise, selfless, and peaceful as the enlightened Buddha himself, and that we can contribute these sublime qualities to the world. In fact, the living flame of enlightenment in Buddhism has many extant or contemporary living masters, and I myself have observed how my masters lived and how they practiced what they preached.

Buddha considered himself a teacher—not a god descended from above or an avatar emanated from another dimension—who found a way to enlightenment or discovered enlightenment in this world and pointed out the way to others. He said, "I, the teacher, am like a doctor. My teachings of Dharma practice and path are like medicine, and the followers are like a community of patients. It is up to the patients whether they follow the doctor's instructions or not, and whether or not they take the medicine regularly. If the doctor could heal the patients he would, but without the patient's participation through continuing to take the medicine, it is very difficult if not impossible." So Buddhism is not about beliefs and creeds and dogmas; it is about practice, how we live and act, and what we do day to day, moment to moment. Buddhism is not a set of beliefs to subscribe to but a way of life—the way of sane, harmonious, and balanced enlightened living.

Buddhism was established in Tibet during the seventh century CE by the enlightened Indian Tantric sage Padmasambhava, the Lotus-Born Guru, renowned as Guru Rinpoche, or the Most Precious Master. The Tibetan King Trisong Detsen and his young wife, Queen Yeshe Tsogyal, became the Lotus Guru's main disciples and Dharma heirs (spiritual successors). Buddhism became Tibet's state religion during their reign (742–797 CE), committing the country and its inhabitants to the principles of nonviolence, peace, enlightenment, sacred education in the inner/spiritual sciences, interconnectedness, and respect for the environment. With their help, and that of the Indian Dzogchen master

Vimalamitra, the Buddha's teachings spread quickly among the mostly nomadic Tibetans.

The ensuing centuries saw Tibetan Buddhism develop several metaphysical schools, monastic and yogic orders, and Tantric-practice lineages. At one time, there were as many as eight different branches of Tibetan Buddhism, of which four main schools remain today: Geluk (Virtuous Ones), Sakya (Gray Earth), Kagyu (Whispered Lineage), and Nyingma (Ancient Ones). The theory and practice of each school have been passed down in an unbroken lineage so that their essence remains authentic and dynamic to this day. Of the grand old lamas trained in Tibet, few are still living—but a younger generation of able teachers has arisen from the ranks of their students as well as of their own reincarnations (*tulkus*).

Although Buddhism in Tibet has been almost reduced to a tourist attraction by the Chinese Communist government (see the Afterword, "Tibet, the Land of Snows," page 77), its teachings today are taking root all over the world. Since the early 1960s, many Asian Buddhist masters have taken up residence in the West, establishing teaching centers and empowering their students to continue spreading the Buddhadharma—Buddhist wisdom and practice.

TIBETAN BUDDHIST MEDITATION

Buddhism has many *upaya* (skillful means): methods to awaken sentient beings from the sleep of illusion, delusion, and suffering. Three "enlightenment trainings"—ethics, meditation, and wisdom/love— are included in the teaching of the Noble Eightfold Path, originating with the Buddha 2,500 years ago and commonly found in all Buddhist schools today. Beyond the scope of this program, you can read more about the Noble Eightfold Path in my book *Awakening the Buddha Within* or in several of the other books listed in the Additional Resources section (page 95).

Dzogchen meditation is one of many methods of Buddhist meditation. Each of the schools and lineages of Buddhism emphasizes certain aspects of spiritual practice in differing proportions. All of these *yanas* (vehicles or paths), if intelligently utilized, deliver us to nirvana.

In Tibetan Buddhism, the main types of essential meditation are Dzogchen and *mahamudra* (the Ultimate Perspective). These are fundamentally awareness practices. These meditation techniques are often supported by other varieties of practice, using different levels of form, symbolism, and energy. Some of these are devotional practices such as guru yoga (merging hearts and minds with the enlightened master or Buddha); visualization meditations (involving meditation deities or spiritual archetypes through a contemplative process of creative imagination); compassion and loving-kindness meditations; *bodhichitta* (the unselfish, compassionate, awakened mind); *tonglen* (exchanging oneself for others); *phowa* (consciousness transference); healing meditations and longevity practices; chanting meditations (using mantras and ritual instruments); breathing and energy meditations, and related Tantric practices; physical yogic meditations; dream yoga (lucid dreaming); bardo yoga (death preparation); clear light meditation; inner heat yoga; spiritual fasting; contemplative prayer; sacred dance and ritual practice; and epistemological debate as mind training to bring about attitude transformation.

Of these many practices, many Tibetan lamas have said that Dzogchen is the ultimate form of meditation, and that—due to its profound simplicity and its radical approach to directly accessing the buddha within—it is especially suited for our turbulent, difficult times. There are practitioners of Dzogchen, the Dalai Lama included, among all four schools of Tibetan Buddhism. It is renowned as "the view from above" because of its vast scope and profound depth. Dzogchen is also known as the "Luminous Heart of the Dharma," the "Radiant Great Perfection," and the "Natural Innate Completeness."

As a practice that traditionally has been taught through oral transmission from a teacher who has received oral transmission from an established lineage holder of the tradition, these practices are also especially suited for a program such as this one, which incorporates not only written information about the practices involved, but also the direct energy and sound vibrations of the teacher's voice on a CD giving personal guided practices, passed on by a living lama who received these instructions through the ancient, tried-and-true initiatory process of oral transmission.

2

THE FOUNDATION OF DZOGCHEN
The Innate Great Perfection

❧

My own mind is Buddha, but I never realize this.
Discursive thoughts are Dharmakaya [ultimate reality],
but I don't realize this.
This is the unfabricated, innate natural state, but I cannot keep to this.
Naturalness is things as they really are, but I have no conviction in this.
Guru, think of me; gaze quickly upon me with compassion.

—JAMGON KONGTRUL I (NINETEENTH CENTURY, TIBET)

In Dzogchen it is taught that we are all buddhas by nature, and we only need to awaken to this fact to realize who and what we truly are. Momentary delusions and confusions obscure our true nature, including our luminous heart, the bodhichitta, the awakened heart-mind-body consciousness that is within us all. It is taught that our sole spiritual task is to directly experience this awakening to our true nature, which is known as enlightenment. This is the essence of self-realization and spiritual illumination, and also the meaning of *satori* (breakthough), as they call it in Japanese Zen. What we need to awaken to and recognize is that what we truly are is our infinitely open and insubstantial luminous true buddha mind, and that the nature of our heart and mind is empty open-awareness and innate wakefulness—whether we know it or not. Dzogchen teaches that this realization cannot be understood intellectually or studied mentally, but it can be transmitted and realized from teacher to student through oral transmission. It cannot be taught, exactly, but as I like to say, although it cannot be taught, it can be caught. Contact with a genuine teacher can facilitate this awakening.

Dzogchen teaches that if we practice today, we will awaken today, and if we practice tonight, we will awaken tonight. But, as contradictory as it may seem, Dzogchen also teaches that we need to apply total dedication and assiduous practice to our highest capacities and sharpest faculties. In other words, although we are complete and perfect as we are, most of us will need to practice over a period of time to completely realize our innate perfection and the inherent freedom and inner peace of natural being.

Since the beginningless beginning, these teachings have been passed on from master to disciple via the renowned spiritual shock tactic called "direct introduction to the nature of mind." This is an initiatory teaching or profound provocation whereby someone introduces us to the truth that we are not just who we think we are and helps us to awaken to all that we are and can be. In this practice, we actualize Buddha's promise that we can all be as enlightened, awakened, wise, loving, and selfless as the Buddha became if we undertake and accomplish the same spiritual journey.

Dzogchen Buddhism is very scientific in a funny way. It teaches that if we can replicate the experiment we can reproduce the results, regardless of whether we are old or young, literate or illiterate, male or female, white, black, yellow, red, multicolored, blind, deaf, or dumb. It teaches that any of us can become enlightened and awakened—not by just believing it is so, but by practicing and realizing the truth for ourselves. Millions have done so over the centuries. These practices are the tried-and-true tools that we can carry with us to awaken ourselves and the world: an inner science of transformation, a spiritual technology for transforming ourselves and transforming the world, for healing ourselves and healing the world.

In order for this liberating realization to become an unshakeable experiential knowing of this sublime inner realization, Dzogchen teachings and practices included in this program provide direct access to this inner treasure. Whether we seek enlightenment or merely hope to spread peace and sanity in the world, Dzogchen can help us bring timeless wisdom to bear on the practical problems of daily life. Best of all, it is a practice anyone can learn and apply right now.

VIEW, MEDITATION, AND ACTION

The great completeness of Dzogchen is always taught as consisting of three parts—view (outlook), meditation (practice), and action or conduct (embodiment in life). The first of these—the Dzogchen view, or sacred perspective—is a clear-sighted, no-holds-barred vision of things unfolding exactly as they are, in which nothing is missing and nothing is added or removed. Everything is seen to be as infinite as boundless space: radiant, immaculate, and stainless from the beginningless beginning. The second part—Dzogchen meditation—is the practice of deepening the view that we have glimpsed. Dzogchen meditation is one of inseparable awareness and emptiness: a naked, luminous, innate wakefulness and openness that is imperturbable, like a mountain. And the third aspect—or action—is of enlightened, beneficial buddha activity that is naturally arising, spontaneous, proactive, compassionate, and appropriate to the conditions and circumstances of everyday life. These three elements represent the fundamental ground of Dzogchen. From this ground springs the path—an ancient, profound, and powerful process of spiritual transformation and awakening—and the fruition of this path is enlightenment in this very lifetime. I myself have seen it.

Traditionally, it is taught in Dzogchen that the view is like the sky, that meditation is like a mountain, and that the spontaneously arising actions and conduct are the Buddha's offspring—innumerable and inexhaustible, like the ocean's waves.

The Dzogchen view is like the sky in that it is infinite, vast, open, and without corners or center. It is a circle whose center is everywhere and whose circumference is nowhere.

Dzogchen meditation is seen as mountainlike in that as we get used to seeing things as they truly are—and leaving them as they are and resting in the natural flow of the Great Perfection—our innate wakefulness becomes imperturbable and unshakeable, unaffected by whatever happens. Through meditation, we get used to resting in the view and abiding in the view; we begin to rely on the view and at the same time see if there is anything deeper or higher or truer than this view; and, if there is, we are naturally drawn to that instead. Thus we ascertain deepening certainty in the view, of things just as they are.

From the combination of the view of the great completeness with the meditation practice of resting in and seeing things as they truly are, spontaneous buddha activity of the Great Perfection naturally arises. And by learning how to sustain this awareness—strengthened in meditation—we are naturally led to inexhaustible, selfless, loving, beneficial buddha activity completely in accord with our present conditions, never getting lost in the action itself or forgetting who and what we truly are, even in the process of doing—just as the ocean never leaves its bed, regardless of whether there are waves or not. This Dzogchen action is not contrived, premeditated, reactive activity, driven by karma, but the proactive, unconditional, liberating buddha activity of the Great Perfection, beyond notions of doer and deed.

The natural result of this threefold path is perfect realization and the complete actualization of the Great Perfection, Dzogchen, in the form of spontaneous and inexhaustible buddha-activity, beneficial to all. Emaho!

THE RAINBOW BODY OF PERFECT ENLIGHTENMENT

In Tibetan, this realization of the true nature of our heart-mind is called *tukarpo*, or the universal panacea, which brings about what is known as the rainbow body of perfect enlightenment. Tibetan Buddhism and Dzogchen masters often describe this rainbow body of perfect enlightenment as the full realization of all possible wisdoms and dimensions of reality at the heart of all manifestation. This rainbow body of perfect enlightenment is not a matter of feeling better, of living forever, or even of overcoming our dissatisfaction and anxiety and suffering, but the genuine realization of the timeless, ageless dimension of totality's pure radiance. It is through this realization that we can become a liberating force, a beacon of light, and a guide to all of those in need.

This rainbow body of perfect enlightenment is not an illusion or fantasy but a mystical experience of the totality of existence—including ourselves—as pure and perfect rainbow light from the beginningless beginning, far beyond the dualities of self and other, form and emptiness, delusion and enlightenment, samsara and nirvana. Seen in this way, there is nothing to wait for and/or hurry toward. Everything is one in the underlying spacious luminosity in which all appears and eventually dissolves, and nothing is separate from this overarching totality.

In this ultimate analysis, there is absolutely nothing else to become wise, knowledgeable, or enlightened about other than our complete interconnectedness with the totality of the universe. However, there are plenty of relative realizations and insights, lessons and understandings that can be gleaned and gathered along the way.

3

THE DZOGCHEN ORAL TRADITION

*The pointing-out instruction is your present
wakefulness pointed out as it is.*

—TULKU URGYEN RINPOCHE

Dzogchen pointing-out instructions and pith instructions are oral instructions given as direct introductions to our true nature and the nature of our heart-mind. They are traditionally received through an interaction with a lama or teacher who has been given a direct introduction through his or her own teacher or teachers.

These oral teachings have come down to us from the Buddha and from even before the Buddha—from primordial truth, imaged as the primordial Buddha—from time immemorial, through an unbroken oral transmission lineage of yogic teachings and pith instructions passed from master to disciple. I have received these teachings from my own enlightened lineage masters. Most of these masters are gone now, reborn in the Himalayas they tell me. But they are always with me, and we are never apart. I feel one with them always.

These teachings are sometimes called "whispered oral transmissions" or secret teachings, although they are always evident to those who are ready to appreciate them, because our true nature is not a thing outside of ourselves that we need to acquire or obtain from a shopping channel or a Tibetan boutique. Go on pilgrimage if you like; a pilgrimage certainly broadens the heart and the soul. But the true inner Himalaya, the secret Tibet, is to awaken to the high ground within—the luminous clarity, the joyous awareness, the total and pure presence known as *rigpa* (nondual total awareness). Innate freedom and perfection are always within our own hearts and minds, available to those of us who can awaken to them.

I am now passing these teachings on to the next generation with the hope and aspiration that you, too, may benefit. May you awaken from the dream and illusion of helplessness, confusion, delusion, misery, suffering, victimhood, self-centered striving, and the dreams of limited egoic separate selfhood to realize the great oneness that is beyond notions of one or many. This is true presence—the interconnectedness and emptiness inseparable, the luminous web of inter-being.

POINTING-OUT INSTRUCTIONS

Although much emphasized in Vajrayana Buddhism, pointing-out instructions are common to all schools of Buddhism in one form or another. These pointing-out instructions include the personal, lessonlike instructions teachers pass on to their students and disciples, like parents introducing their children to life in its intimate details, without relying on books or scripture, history, ritual, or philosophical treatises and texts. These pointing-out instructions—also known as the introduction to the nature of mind—are transrational, suddenly impactful transmissions from mind to mind and heart to heart, intent upon shocking the disciple into wakefulness on the spot, through recognition of the true nature of heart-mind as buddha mind.

Ever since the time of the siddhas (spiritual adepts) in ancient India, these pointing-out instructions have been especially important in the transmission of Mahamudra and Dzogchen, especially in the Kagyu-Nyingma school in which I am an authorized and transmitted lama. In this lineage, we do not rely much on debate, logic, philosophy, or monasticism to teach the dialectics of emptiness (*shunyata*), but more directly on the actual experience of the Great Perfection through meditation, empowerment, initiation, and Tibetan yoga practices. In this way, the use of pointing-out instructions is designed to provoke a sudden awakening sooner rather than later. In Dzogchen, we traditionally introduce this experience from master to disciple in person, as I am endeavoring to do in this program, through a combination of teachings and guided Dzogchen practices on the enclosed CD. Pointing-out instructions are part of each of the individual meditations included. Please try to pay attention; it pays off.

What we call the mind-to-mind or heart-to-heart transmission—what I like to call mouth-to-mouth spiritual resuscitation, or in this case mouth-to-ear spiritual resuscitation—is a vibrating resource between teacher and student that can then be applied to your individual meditation practice. The master-induced awakening or glimpse of reality can then be used for guidance or reference, or as a pole star as it were. In this perspective, the breakthrough or recognition of shunyata or the buddha nature of one's own heart and mind is not the end of the path, but the beginning of the true path, for which we now have some guidance and a direction to follow. It is as if for a moment we have experienced the sun breaking through the clouds, but then the clouds suddenly cover up the sun again, as our habitual patterns and obscurations cover up our luminous true nature. However, having had that glimpse, we know that there is a sun because we have seen it, and we understand that there is light in the world even on a cloudy day. We can recognize the difference between day and night and understand why. It is an essentially different relationship than the one we experienced when we were growing up and were told to believe that there is a God in heaven, or that Buddha is sitting somewhere in nirvana.

There is no substitute for the actual epiphanic experience, through which we come to know that there actually is a *there* there. This experience alone uproots many of the illusions and doubts we have about the nature of reality. And since we have actually experienced this breakthrough event for ourselves—or we have at least had a glimpse of what we are searching for—our awareness, understanding, and perspective (our view or outlook) fundamentally changes, just as we do not need to see the sun all the time in order to know that it exists, even behind the clouds or in darkness. And, as the poet Kabir sang, "I glimpsed it for fifteen seconds and it made me a servant for life."

PITH INSTRUCTIONS

When I first received the pith instructions,
I had the urge to gulp it all at once,
like a starving man face-to-face with food.
—PATRUL RINPOCHE

The Dzogchen view is often taught via pith instructions, or the quintessential elixir of mind-meditation teachings boiled down from the essence of empty awareness practice. The essence of these pith instructions on the view is to help us to see things as they are while seeing through them at the same time and to avoid being deceived by the mere appearances of phenomena and noumena (mind-stuff). In this practice, the essence of emptiness and awareness is insepara- ble—we see things as they arise and dissolve, but we also at the same time see through them into their insubstantial, empty, open, radiant, and marvelous nature. These pith instructions are not only helpful in meditation practice but are also applicable and integrable into daily life. Pith instructions are used to open the chapters in this book, and many of the main instructions are also included in the Addendum (page 81). Some of the most important of these pith instructions are:

Just as it is.

—

Let go and let be.

—

Seeing through, being through.

—

What we seek, we are.

—

Not too tight or too loose.

—

Take the Vajra shortcut.

—

Direct access.

—

Nowness/immediacy.

—

Leave it as it is, and rest your weary mind.

—

Naturalness is the way.
Natural mind is buddha mind.

—

We are all buddhas; we only have to recognize that fact.

—

Everything is pure and spontaneously accomplished from the outset.

—

Nothing to do and nowhere to go.

—

Seeing, recognizing, penetrating, releasing.

—

See through the seer and be free.

—

Nothing to do but remain in the View.

—

Pure vision: see the buddha in everyone and everything.

These pith instructions are known in Tibetan as *men-ngak* and in Sanskrit as *upadesha.* These essence words are the highest direct words, the pithy pointers, what we call in Tibetan *mar-tri,* or red guidance, naked words. Or, let us say, naked truth. These pith instructions are not just the information that we have read in books or the Buddhist scriptures, but are the essence of lessons actually learned from life, the most naked instructions boiled down to their essence or pith. They are, in a sense, concentrated wisdom—the way a vitamin C pill contains 1,000 milligrams of ascorbic acid so that we do not have to eat dozens of oranges to get enough of the active ingredient.

In this way, pith instructions are the boiled-down elixir of all of the wisdom teachings of enlightenment that have been passed down and preserved orally until modern times. Their essence is not something written down but lived as the oral living flame of enlightenment. Pith instructions are like a flame of truth being passed from one candle to another, from my teacher to me to you—the same flame but different wax and bodies. This is how we pay back our spiritual benefactors and masters—those to whom we are so grateful—by realizing this innate wisdom and cherishing it, and then practicing it and passing it on intact to those who are capable of upholding it. Motivation and skillful means are important—we must pass it on for the right reasons at the right time.

One example of how this oral tradition of personal instruction operates is how my own teacher—the late Khyentse Rinpoche—told me that, in Dzogchen, there are two common mistakes or faults for the experienced meditator: one is that you let go too soon, but the other is that you let go too late. Now, "letting go" is very much advised in Buddhist meditation, and this instruction to let go is often included in these pith instructions; but Khyentse Rinpoche said that if you let go too soon, you will not persevere and go through the difficulties and lessons it is necessary to go through. But, on the other hand, you can also let go too late and become attached to the technique and hold onto it well beyond its proper use, like someone on an airplane that is stuck in a holding pattern, never lands, and thus cannot continue on with the journey. In the Buddha's original teachings, he says that the Dharma teachings are like a raft to carry us across the boiling ocean of sorrow, suffering, and confusion, but we do not have to keep carrying the raft on our shoulders when we have reached the far shore. So, the essential insight in this particular pith instruction is not to be too technique-oriented, mistaking the means for the end or being afraid to let go of the technique and grow or move on to what may be next.

One of my favorite pith instructions comes from the gentle and wise Lama Jamgon Kongtrul Lodro Thaye, the "infinite brilliant intellect." He said there were four deviations from the view: "It is too close, so we overlook it; it seems too good to be true, so we cannot believe it; it is too profound, so we cannot fathom it; it is not outside ourselves, so we cannot attain it anew." Whatever you want to call "it," whatever we seek—God, our true nature, buddha-nature—it is not outside ourselves, so we overlook it.

These pith instructions often address fundamental human questions about the true nature of our heart-mind, who we are, and what is real. They also attempt to answer other questions about the nature of God, the soul, the afterlife, birth and death, and the purpose and meaning of life. They also speak of our true relation with the ultimate, the relationship between the impermanent and the eternal, the relationship between God and humanity, and what we are all doing here.

TALES OF ENLIGHTENMENT

Hearing or reading the biographies of illumined spiritual masters teaches us their wisdom and enlightened way of life. Simply to hear of the lives of such living buddhas can bring one onto the path of liberation.

—DILGO KHYENTSE RINPOCHE

Tales from the heart enter the heart, instilling both wisdom and compassionate action. The reflection upon what are known as enlightenment stories is another important teaching and transmission aspect of the Tibetan tradition. Through repeating these stories, we enter into and catch the great wave of blessings and inspiration from all of those masters who have gone before us—the entire invisible array of the ascendant *sangha* (community) that accompanies true practitioners always. The purpose of these tales—through preserving and transmitting what the actual circumstances and experiences of enlightenment have been and are—is to provoke, instruct, motivate, edify, and amuse, and eventually lead to spiritual awakening.

Some of these enlightenment stories have been written down, but most of them are found exclusively in the oral tradition. I myself have collected and translated 158 such stories in *The Snow Lion's Turquoise Mane: Wisdom Tales from Tibet*, an anthology of Himalayan teaching tales. For example, there are stories of the iconoclastic, turn-of-the-last-century "enlightened vagabond" Patrul Rinpoche of Dzogchen Monastery in Kham; tales of Bhutan's crazy-wise master Drukpa Kunley, whose songs are matched in profundity by their profanity; and other stories of how ordinary people woke up and realized truth and reality.

I often find it useful to teach about the impeccable monk and learned abbot Naropa and the crazy-wise adept Tilopa, the greatest Tantric yogi of his time, who lived over a thousand years ago in northern India. Tilopa spent over twelve years challenging his disciple Naropa in every possible way, including twelve great hardships, until one day Naropa was sitting on the ground in front of him and Tilopa hit him in the face with his filthy sandal. Naropa woke up to supreme and total enlightenment right there and then and sang a song of enlightenment on the spot, describing that the guru's heart-mind, Buddha's heart-mind, and his were one and the same and had always been the same. This essential truth was something that Naropa had not experienced no matter how much he had studied the Buddhist scriptures and philosophies; it required Tilopa's outrageous nonverbal pointing-out instruction—with a blow—for Naropa to awaken to all that was within him.

This transmission from Tilopa to Naropa has been passed down to us for over a thousand years, and it is still happening today. An American friend of mine who was an ordained Buddhist nun for thirteen years (and is now a lama herself) tells the story of how her lama repeatedly avoided introducing her to the nature of mind. And then, one day, while they were sitting silently side by side in the monastery garden, he suddenly shouted and clapped his hands, and she received a direct transmission that was far more profound and powerful than any previous teachings. Let me point out that this happened in New York state, not in faraway Tibet. Awakening is not something that happens only thousands of miles away or happened only hundreds of years ago to people of a different skin color.

The point is not necessarily that Buddhists should be hitting people in the face with our shoes or shouting at them, but these are a few examples of the kind of shock tactics included in these tales of enlightenment that historical lineage masters have successfully used to break through their students' hardened conceptual frameworks to transport them far beyond themselves and back to who and what they truly are. This is known as the introduction to the nature of mahamudra—a transmission of the nature of mind in which there is nothing to transmit and nothing to receive, for it is realized in the moment to be all within.

Naropa's great awakening eventually led him to teach others, including Milarepa's guru, Marpa the Translator. Marpa brought these teachings to Tibet in the eleventh century, setting in motion a renewed wave of enlightened practice, the results of which have been passed down to us today—through Tilopa to Naropa, and from Naropa through Marpa to Milarepa, and descending through the centuries through the lineage of the Karmapas. Later the transmission was also given to the Dalai Lama and other grand lamas of the various schools and lineages in Tibet.

My late guru and root lama, Dilgo Khyentse Rinpoche, often explained the nature of the mind as like a mirror or crystal. When seen from one side, it is transparent—from the other side, everything is reflected clearly. It can radiate light and color without itself changing or moving. The mind is also like a crystal in that it is transparent and empty of color, but it immediately takes on the color and hue of whatever is near it and radiates all of the colors of the rainbow when a light beam passes through it. This is the intrinsic nature of mind, he taught: empty and transparent yet radiant, lucid and sparkling, and inexhaustibly and spontaneously manifesting the entire world and all of our experiences.

One day in the 1980s, Khyentse Rinpoche directly introduced me to the intrinsic nature of mind or mind essence by holding up a radiant crystal, gesturing toward it menacingly and symbolically with one large gold ring finger, and suddenly exclaiming in a shockingly loud voice, "What is mind?" With this, he shocked me into another way of being and seeing in which his buddha heart-mind, the Buddha's heart-mind, and my heart-mind were obviously not two, not three, but one and inseparable. And I knew that this heart-mind was not localized anywhere but active everywhere, and I had never been apart from it even when I was not aware of it. This is one example of the direct, mind-to-mind, heart-to-heart, and mouth-to-ear oral tradition of the Dzogchen lineage often included in tales of enlightenment.

From the parentlike guru to the childlike disciple, often amidst an elaborate Tantric ritual, there is often just this type of breakthrough or spiritual epiphany in the student—if we are attentive, if our karma is ripe, and if we have an authentic connection with that lineage master. These breakthroughs take us beyond body and mind, beyond all dualisms of self and other, beyond samsara and nirvana, beyond master and disciple. When such an august Tibetan elder and master—truly one of the great hierarchs of the ancient traditions of the earth—shouts a short, shocking question right into your face while you are in a meditative state of mind and devotionally exposed and truly open, it is a thousand times more profound than when a skilled jeweler taps a fine diamond so that the jewel breaks open along its perfect flaws and reveals its beauties within. This kind of spiritual shock tactic or introduction to the nature of mind is so profound and powerful that it produces a spiritual jewel infinitely more lustrous and valuable.

Another master with whom I studied used to pound on a table or clap his hands loudly at a crucial moment to introduce us to the intrinsic nature of mind. Sometimes he would ask, "Who is hearing? Who is experiencing?" The first time that he did this, I experienced his mind and mine not as separate but as the ultimate reality, and it felt like everything that was arising in my mind was likewise present in his and the Buddha's mind as well. Mysteriously, it felt as if his words were coming out of my own mouth.

Even now I have to ask myself, is that not the case right now? Are these things arising within me really me and mine—my thoughts and feelings, my body, my concerns, and my neuroses? In actuality, it is all the body of the Buddha—the shadows are nothing but light. Emaho, fantastic! Thank you, Master Rinpoche: what a wonderful teaching and transmission you have given me for all time.

Different Dharma masters have their own skillful means and methods to awaken beings to reality. My first Dzogchen master in Darjeeling in the early 1970s was the venerable Kangyur Rinpoche (1897–1975). He was the father of my mentor Tulku Pema Wang-yal, a wonderful English-speaking Kagyu-Nyingma lama who now lives in France and is the resident master of our three-year Dzogchen retreats there. Kangyur Rinpoche was a very powerful enlightened master, who used to wake up disciples with provocative words and symbolic gestures. He would ask his close students to look directly into this immediate moment to see what color, what shape, what size was their mind, and in what location the heart-mind was to be found, often initiating a spiritual awakening and insight.

In these tales of enlightenment, sudden provocation or master-induced epiphany often brings one to a nonconceptual realization of the true nature of primordial identity. This realization is far beyond one's self and any notion of self, and beyond no-self and selflessness, too. It is a realization of shunyata, or the luminous void. We can see the essence of this realization in countless Zen stories about sudden enlightenment experiences (*satori*). There is a sudden awakening to who and what we truly are as the "knowing one"—a total presence of innate awareness. As the Tibetans say, better than knowing hundreds and thousands of things is to know the one thing that frees and liberates all. This truth has been Buddha's inmost teaching from the beginning: that it is all within, that we are all buddhas by nature, and we just have to realize it.

4

NATURAL MEDITATION

꿇

*One instant of total awareness is one instant of
perfect freedom and enlightenment.*
—THE WISDOM DEITY, MANJUSHRI

Some people think meditating is closing your eyes and trying not
to think, or that meditation is simply a process to calm and clear
the mind. That is known as concentrative meditation, or tranquility
meditation—a process of creating a special focused state of mind like
light or bliss, hearing a celestial sound, or saying a certain mantra.
Buddhist meditation practices also include loving-kindness meditations, meditations on compassion, healing meditations, visualization
meditations, and many other kinds of meditative disciplines, which
you can learn elsewhere.

All forms of mindfulness meditation—the practice of observing
things as they are—are "natural" in the sense that they bring us back
to our present experience: reality. In the context of this program,

however, "natural meditation" refers specifically to Dzogchen meditation. Practically speaking, the function of Dzogchen meditation is to awaken naked awareness—a state that exists beyond the realm of conceptual forms, culture, or belief systems.

The essence of Dzogchen meditation is called *rangshar rangdrol* in Tibetan ("by itself arising," "by itself liberating/releasing"). Thus one appreciates the empty yet luminous, vividly appearing form of all created things, outer and inner. Thus, natural meditation is not a process of suppressing thoughts or feelings, nor of being carried away by them, but of simply becoming aware of their spontaneous, unhindered display, their arising and passing on, moment to moment. Like a surfer riding ocean waves, the Dzogchen practitioner does not try to iron out the waves of thought and perception, to flatten out the mind, or to flatline the brain waves. As a skilled surfer knows, the bigger the waves, the better the surfing. For the meditator, it is a process of enjoying the blissful awareness of seeing through things as they arise, and, like the floats in an Easter parade going by, the more the merrier and the better the show. Through this awareness, we can enjoy the process and know that it is just a show by enjoying the display while simultaneously remaining unentangled by it. Tilopa said that it is not outer things but inner clinging and fixation that entangle us.

Dzogchen meditation is based on three vital points: first, natural body as Buddha's body; second, natural breath and energy as Buddha's breath and energy; and, finally, natural heart and mind as Buddha's heart-mind. The instructions are the same in each case; leave it as it is. This acceptance of what is *as it is* helps us to balance effort and noneffort in our practice of the natural Great Perfection.

Therefore, in Dzogchen meditation we practice natural body, natural breath and energy, and natural heart-mind—the "three naturals"—combined with leaving things as they are, letting be, letting things come and go, seeing things as they are and not as we would like them to be—and certainly not as they are not. With practice, we get used to trusting the ongoing flow and lawful karmic unfolding of things when we simply leave them as they are. We see that things may be empty of solid substantial reality, but they continue to manifest and affect other things, which are also empty of solid substantial reality but have their own effects, which also have to be considered.

In Dzogchen meditation, we witness the continual magical display, moment after moment—like poem after poem, or celestial song after celestial song, what Hindus call the divine dance, *maya* or *lila*—of the dance of illusion, arising and continuing and yet without any independent, lasting, substantial solidity or reality. We do not have to suppress or change this continual magical display, but we can recognize it for what it is—our own projections as the display of intrinsic awareness.

Thus, Dzogchen meditation is not really doing anything, which is why it is called nonmeditation or beyond meditation. A Tibetan text refers to it as "Buddhahood without meditating." In other words, Dzogchen meditation is a process of recognizing our true nature in every moment, not just by crossing our legs and paying attention to our breath, but by deep, penetrating insight and discriminating awareness that discerns the true nature of things as they are.

Nonaction in this context also means not constructing special states of mind, altering and manipulating our minds, or trying to pretty up the picture or to have better moods. It is not to be distracted by breath counting or prayers and mantras, or by merely daydreaming and being carried away by endless chains of discursive thought and feeling. Instead, it requires becoming aware of the nature of thought or perception itself. The practitioner should not be wandering around in the past, resurrecting thoughts that are dead and gone, or in fantasy, concerned with thoughts about the future, about what is yet to come.

Natural meditation is also a process of letting go of the present—not even being in the present through habitual reference points relating to linear time; but instead living in timeless time, that nowness that sparkles on the edge of infinity: the edge of none-ness and oneness, of being and being nothing, of the luminous void, of the womb of all the buddhas—or the mother of all the buddhas, as it is sometimes called. This is *shunyata* in Sanskrit, sometimes translated as emptiness. But this shunyata is really a luminous emptiness, endowed with the heart of compassion. It is a radiant cognizance, what we call the infinite radiance and wisdom of the natural Great Perfection. It is a luminous openness that is our divine core, our buddha nature. And just as great peace is beyond the dualism of peace and quiet, inner stillness is beyond the dualism of stillness and movement—our inner center remains unchanged. When we are centered, settled, and balanced, we can be at peace at any speed, at any decibel level.

One of my own teachers, the late great Kalu Rinpoche—the Dalai Lama's yoga teacher and the senior meditation master of the Kagyu lineage—taught in this meditation practice that we should allow all thoughts, feelings, and perceptions to settle like snowflakes falling into a clear lake. We do not have to get rid of them or wash them away or stop them, but only to see how they settle and dissolve naturally by themselves without any effort on our parts, just as everything appears and eventually disappears. In this way, we learn how to drop our physical attachments and clinging, as well as our clinging to our minds, identities, mental attachments, preoccupations, and concerns. And then, as everything that can fall away does fall away, we can simply rest in the luminous clarity and bliss of total naked awareness itself, the groundless ground of incandescent being. Dzogchen meditation is not any form of thinking, analysis, or mental gymnastics, but a natural meditation relying on innate wakefulness and naked, uncontrived awareness. Kalu Rinpoche taught that anyone can become enlightened in this lifetime through such a practice, regardless of age, nationality, gender, how one looks, whether one is learned or not, and so forth.

PRACTICING DZOGCHEN MEDITATION

To practice Dzogchen meditation, it is traditional to select a spot, perhaps outdoors, where you will be undisturbed and will not disturb others. The opening meditations in this program, however, are designed to be done upon first awakening in the morning, and so are best done in bed or nearby, as described later. In these and other situations where you must practice indoors, clear your practice space of any clutter, work-related papers, and so on. If you cannot face a window through which you can see the sky, try at least to create the atmosphere of a natural environment and clean spaciousness in the places where you practice meditation.

Most of the guided meditation practices on the enclosed CD are done sitting on the ground, in a cross-legged position. Many people choose to sit on a firm cushion. If your legs are flexible enough, you might want to sit in a full- or half-lotus position, with one or both feet resting on the opposite thigh. If necessary, you can sit in a chair. A beach chair or recliner will work for outdoor meditation.

Take time to find your balance until you feel stable, like a pyramid. Remaining erect in this dignified position, allow yourself to relax completely. Always begin with a sense of appreciation and delight.

Three principles should be applied to your meditation: relaxing, arriving and centering, and naturalness. To relax in this context is to surrender any tendency to control or manipulate the situation in which you find yourself. Simply settle into the present moment and let go of thoughts, feelings, memories, and plans about work, school, family, or friends. Let go of the past and future, and practice entering the now, right on the spot. Sit on the Buddha's seat, and let him do it; there is nothing more for you to do for now.

The second stage of meditation is to arrive. This means to bring your entire being into complete, unified presence. No part of you is wandering somewhere else, in thoughts of past or future. You are 100 percent present, mindful, attentive.

The third principle—naturalness—refers to letting everything be as it is. It could be said that naturalness encompasses both relaxing and arriving: surrendering to the moment and becoming a part of it. Naturalness goes further, however, in that you fully accept yourself, exactly as you are: a buddhalike being, complete and perfect just as you are, a Bodhisattva practicing for the ultimate benefit of one and all.

The meditation practices included on Tracks 1 through 7 on the enclosed CD are designed to be practiced separately after reading the instructions for each meditation and before going on to the next practice. Once you have practiced each of the meditations, you can at any time return to them individually or practice a selection of the individual practices in one sitting. Once you feel familiar with the individual practices, you can practice them on your own without the guided instructions. When you do, my advice is to extend the meditations to the limit that you feel you can easily maintain as a daily practice—traditionally thirty to sixty minutes. Later, if you so choose, you can also perform all seven guided practices in sequence from beginning to end. In this way, the CD becomes a complete guided and well-rounded eighty-minute Dzogchen meditation practice.

❉ LISTEN TO TRACK 3 *Natural Meditation*

Now, to begin your Dzogchen meditation practice, find a comfortable seat and listen to Track 3 on the enclosed CD, where I will guide you through a session of natural meditation. When you have completed the program and are ready to perform the seven meditations as part of a daily practice, this particular meditation is best performed as the third part of your daily practice, which is why it appears in that position.

5

MORNING WAKE-UP SKY BREATH PRACTICE

Let your awareness become heightened:
Let it spread out into the infinite sky.
From that state of complete openness,
That vast expanse, sing out!

—LAMA SHABKAR

THE "AH" MANTRA

Buddhist spirituality is all about awakening. In fact, the word "buddha" comes from the root "bodhi," to awaken or to wake up. So it is appropriate to greet the day with the Dzogchen morning wake-up Sky Breath practice. For this practice, we use the easy-to-memorize, user-friendly, Dzogchen Sky Breath mantra "AH." Although this is traditionally practiced first thing in the morning, you can also take any moment in the day to wake yourself up and to awaken to the world, or simply to refresh and energize yourself. I find that stopping in the midst of a busy trip to simply take a deep breath and exhale with a great releasing "Aaaah" can perforate the solidity and claustrophobia of an intense day, letting the fresh air of spirit and awareness blow through.

To chant the "AH" mantra, take a deep breath and on your exhalation open your eyes and mouth wide, raise your gaze, and chant a resounding, relieving "Aaaah" as far as you can go. Be aware of your out-breath as you chant the mantra, and repeat the mantra from one to three times. You can try to chant at different volumes and in different tones, emptying yourself totally and dissolving with each out-breath. As you do this, be aware of how your mind unites and mingles with space and how that space itself mingles with your awareness. Let everything else—thoughts, emotions, feelings, plans, distractions, noises, expectations—dissolve in vast, open space. Simply rest in the view, at ease with everything, including yourself, precisely as you are.

At the end of your exhalation, let the sound of the mantra "AH" resound into nothingness, both within and without, and rest in the utter silence and simplicity of the natural state of just being. When thoughts arise into this state of natural meditation, chant a few lengthy "AHs," following the out-breath. Try to become aware of dissolving a little more with each "AH" repetition. Then, once again, rest in the spacious openness and clarity of natural meditation. You can continue to alternate this dissolving and resting at your own pace, in your own natural way.

❋ LISTEN TO TRACK 1 *Morning Wake-Up Sky Breath Practice*

I have included a guided session of this practice incorporated into a morning wake-up routine as Track One on the enclosed CD. Once you feel comfortable with the practice as taught on the CD, you are free to adapt it for your own use. Do not feel obligated to perform this only as part of your morning practice! The big exhalation called Sky Breath with the mantra "AH" can be used at any time, in any situation, when you feel the need for a little spaciousness or simply the need to wake up and become more alert and aware. If you are in public and do not feel comfortable chanting the "AH" mantra out loud, you can perform it inwardly, to yourself, while riding a great out-breath.

PRACTICING THE MORNING WAKE-UP SKY BREATH PRACTICE ON YOUR OWN

As taught as part of the guided practice: when you wake in the morning, before you get out of bed, sit up and join the soles of your feet together, toes to toes, heels to heels. Then, with your first in-breath, reach your arms up over your head, point your fingers toward the sky, and, with a big out-breath, say "Aaaah." Then take another deep in-breath and bring your hands down to your knees. Your posture remains the same—with your feet pressed together, your head upraised, your eyes closed, and your hands on your knees. Take a few deep breaths in this position and release, letting everything just be in the Great Perfection of this moment of Dzogchen, the fresh first instant, dawn of creation. You can repeat this process three times, but once is enough.

Then carefully, mindfully, attentively, get out of bed and stand with your hands at your side and your feet flat on the floor. Take a deep breath, relax, and straighten your spine. Then take a deep breath and bring your hands up over your head, open your eyes, look up—not at the ceiling but up at a 45- to 60-degree angle—and reach your fingertips up to the sky, palms out, and chant again, with your eyes open, mouth open, chest open, everything open: "Aaaah." Let your arms fall open with your breath, relax, and smile with your entire luminous rainbow body.

The third posture of the Sky Breath practice is to stand like a mountain or a great tree, rooted in the earth—firm and unshakeable—with your head in the sky and heaven and your feet on the earth, connecting both and stuck in neither, while letting go to experience total energy flow. Rest in this state of natural meditation for as long as you want.

When you have completed your Sky Breath practice, walk gently, attentively, mindfully to your meditation seat or your meditation room. If you need to stop in the bathroom first, do so. In your practice place, you will perform the second step of your Dzogchen meditation practice, called *rushen* or subtle discernment.

The seed syllable "AH" in Tibetan script

6

RUSHEN

꘩

When the empty looks at the empty,
who is there to look at something empty?
—NYOSHUL KHENPO RINPOCHE

Since time immemorial, masters including Socrates have exhorted us to know ourselves. Our human quest for meaning, purpose, and deeper understanding of our true identity and place in life has given birth to all the world's great religions, philosophies, and ethical systems. Self-inquiry is an ancient tool for plumbing the depths and splendor of our own inner nature and actually discovering who and what we truly are. The traditional means of self-inquiry in the Dzogchen tradition is known as rushen.

Rushen has traditionally been a secret practice that consists of two forms, known as inner and outer rushen. Outer rushen is best practiced under the guidance of a teacher because it involves acting out all of the impulses of our karmic imprints or *samskaras*. Inner rushen is a series of incisive, practical, contemplative, and analytical meditation exercises through which we can learn to distinguish the gold of our own buddha nature from the brass of ego and its persona. We discover how to loosen the hold of selfishness and egotistical attachments and fixations, and open wide the doors for the natural buddha within to stand up and shine. Here dawns the inherent freedom and perfection of natural living, of our authentic being—the innate Great Perfection.

But before we can discriminate between different states of mind, we have to first experience the difference between mind with a small "m"—or the conceptual, intellectual, egoic mind or mental consciousness—and the pure presence and innate awareness of Mind with a capital "M." Pure Mind consists of Awareness with a capital "A"—it is not limited personal awareness but incandescent naked Awareness, pure presence, a radiant undivided totality—a transpersonal knowingness, luminous Awareness, an empty open clarity, pure cognizance.

Rushen means subtle discernment through self-inquiry and exhausting karmic conditioning, and it is through rushen that we can discern the true nature of heart and mind and introduce ourselves to the recognition of who and what we truly are. Rushen is naked awareness practice, and it is designed to directly introduce us to the nature of this innate awareness—our immaculate primordial buddha mind—and to recognize it as our true selves. Rushen includes open-ended inquiry that can take us far beyond thoughts and concepts until we arrive at innate wakefulness, pure presence, our groundless and boundless, luminous spiritual nature beyond the illusory conventional self and its machinations. It is through rushen that we come to recognize the innate nature of mind or our buddha nature and come to full awareness in the present moment—without preconceptions about what awareness means or what we can get out of it, without hope and expectation, without fear, anxiety, and disappointment. Rushen helps us to discern the subtle differences between the spontaneous, natural heart-mind or luminous spiritual lucidity—which simply *knows*— and the ego-mind that conceptualizes, separates, strategizes, judges, and manipulates. Rushen helps us to discern between self with a small "s", and our transpersonal being or impersonal Self with a capital "S." It helps us to distinguish between thoughts and thinking on the one hand and mindfulness and awareness on the other, and it teaches us how we can be mindful of thoughts and experiences without becoming entangled in them. It also teaches us how we can distinguish between feelings and mindfulness, and how we can be aware of our feelings and not necessarily be caught up in them. It shows us how to distinguish the natural from the fabricated and contrived, how to discern the difference between doing and being, how to be more in touch with our being, and how to not lose ourselves or our centeredness and pure presence amidst our various doings, even as we continue doing them. Rushen helps us to distinguish between effort and noneffort or that which is beyond effort, what is known as pure and total flow—the Way in Taoism, or nonstriving and nonaction in Tibetan Buddhism. This is the spiritual zone, or, as athletes refer to it, this is like being in the zone where they are one with everything, not thinking and with no need to think. This is the sacred zone, in which everything just flows.

Rushen helps us to discern these and many other subtle distinctions so that we start to find out who and what we truly are and that we are not just who we think we are. We are not a limited body, a personality, an ego structure or history; we are not just a man or a woman, young or old, healthy or sick, not just an American or non-American, not a Buddhist or a Christian or a Jew, or, for that matter, not an agnostic or an atheist.

Once we become aware of what we are not, we begin to uncover and discover who and what we truly are, beyond all such relative distinctions. When we realize our true nature, we enter into the sphere of the luminous Great Perfection. We see that we can, at least for a moment, leave it as it is, rest our weary hearts and minds, and actually let go and relax—finding refuge in this moment: in empty, luminous, uninhibited activity and in the Great Perfection flowing right through us. Right now you may feel far from such high ideals, but I assure you that it is always flowing right through you, and you are never apart from it. The natural perfection path is the all-pervasive ground or greater context from which one can never completely stray.

Following this introduction to the nature of our mind (included as Track 2 on the enclosed CD), I exhort you to do your own introspection and inner, analytical rushen meditation practice. Look into your mind when it is still and when it is moving. Is it the same mind when it is still and when it is moving, or is it two different minds? Look to where your thoughts and feelings arise from, where they are when they are present, and where they go when they dissolve. And, when they dissolve, follow that dissolution point into the luminous void from which everything springs and into which everything returns, the womb of shunyata.

Through this practice of rushen, you will get more deeply in touch with your true self, the groundless ground of your primordial being. You will learn how to let go of your body, how to let go of your thoughts and thinking—not to mention your story and roles in life—to see what happens when you let go of your mind and experience pure presence. There is so much more room for the natural Great Perfection to emerge spontaneously when you get out of your own way!

Everyone has had this experience at some time in their lives. Sometimes it is glimpsed in a moment of sexual ecstasy, or a "cosmic orgasm." It sometimes occurs in states of spiritual epiphany or breakthrough, or in a moment of terror when headlights are coming right at us in the dark. There are actually many moments when the mind stops, and we are simply present, without thought or concept. In those moments, turn the spotlight inward and *look*: Who or what is experiencing your experience? Who or what are you? Who is hearing? Who is thinking; who is feeling; who is reading these words? Who is trying to meditate or control the mind? Who am I? Who is afraid of dying? Who dies? What dies?

With rushen, we analyze and go into all of these questions in order to directly explore the depths of ourselves and the true nature of reality. All things—including the mind—arise from emptiness. Everything is transparent, even when present, and is marked or characterized by emptiness. Everything—including ourselves—is vivid yet insubstantial, like a rainbow. Everything passes; nothing remains. Savor that.

We are not in control of the universe; the universe is forever out of our control. That is the bad news, but it is also the good news; this means we do not have to control it. We can, however, control our own behavior, and our behavior is determined by our level of awareness. As the Buddha said, "If you want to protect your feet, you do not have to cover the whole world with leather; you just have to cover your feet with shoes." This is the spiritual discovery that utterly transforms your experience of the world and your presence in it. It is not what happens to us but what we make of it that makes all the difference.

Rushen is a great way to attain a direct experience of the Great Perfection, because when we find out who and what we truly are—and see through the illusions that we have about who we are and what we are not—we naturally come to realize our true nature. Through this profound inner recognition we not only become free of our illusions, but we also begin to see that same true nature in everyone. Seen in this way, everyone is a luminous spiritual being working it out here on earth in the relative sphere, in the realm of names and forms and bodies and personalities and life roles and positions.

In spite of this, everyone wants and needs the same things, more or less, and everyone is pursuing these same basic desires through different means, which brings about various kinds of conflict. It is at this point that we begin to realize the truth of the Buddhist adage that the main problem with worldly beings is that they think that happiness and sadness come from outside of themselves, whereas the truth is that what we seek can only be found within.

The Dzogchen masters teach that the heart-mind is magnificent in its natural state, and it is best to leave it as it is. This is one of my favorite Dzogchen teachings, because it encourages us to leave everything as it is and to let it all be; it promises that as we come to understand, trust, appreciate, and deeply accept ourselves and the way things are, the more at home and profoundly at peace we can be—wherever we are and with whomever we may be. By learning how to befriend ourselves, we learn how to befriend all; by coming to know ourselves, we come to know and understand all. Thus Milarepa sang, "Having left homeland and family ties behind, now all places are my country, all people my people."

I have included a guided session on rushen as Track 2 on the enclosed CD.

✳ LISTEN TO TRACK 2 *Rushen*

PRACTICING RUSHEN ON YOUR OWN

Once you have practiced rushen along with the guided session on Track Two, you can continue to deepen the practice on your own. The basic instructions for rushen practice are to take a comfortable seat in your meditation room or sacred space, wherever you can practice. You can either sit cross-legged on the floor or in a straight-backed chair or couch, as long as you have a reasonable upright and balanced posture—not leaning back too much or falling asleep. Your backbone is your central channel and it should be as straight as possible so that your vertebrae are aligned one on top of another.

Relax in this posture and take a few deep breaths to calm and clear your mind. Come into an awareness of just sitting, just breathing—letting all else go. Relax and fully inhabit the present moment. Breathe with all your awareness, so that everything else can just go by, with nothing more to figure out, accomplish, keep track of, or achieve. Just be present, attentive, wakeful—mindful of your sitting, your breathing, and the sublime silence, simplicity, and joy of the present moment.

Once your mind is calm, focused, lucid, and clear, abruptly turn the mind on itself—mind the mind and turn it inward, with laserlike self-inquiry questions: "Who is thinking my thoughts?

Who is trying to meditate? Who is it; what is it; where is it? Who is experiencing my experience right now?"

There is no need to analyze too much—just abruptly pop the question and observe what happens. Let go and see if you can startle yourself into a new way of seeing and being, short-circuiting your usual outward-looking, dualistic thought process of self and other. See through the seer, directly experience the experiencer, and be free; rest in luminous centerless openness, the natural Great Perfection, pure presence, rigpa.

Again cutting even deeper, abruptly turn the mind upon itself again: Who is experiencing? Who and what is hearing? Who and what is seeing, thinking, and feeling? Who is having these physical sensations? Who is it; what is it; where is it? Is it in the head; is it in the body; is it in the heart; is it in the mind and consciousness? Who is experiencing? Who or what am I? How is it happening? See if you can enter the bottomless gap between thoughts, beneath thoughts. See if you can directly experience whatever is not thought—the luminous awareness that exists prethought or beyond or beneath thought, or after all thought has ceased. Trace the source of all of your thoughts, feelings, experiences, physical sensations, and perceptions. Notice how they arise, and, after they arise, where they are in your present experience and where they go. See if you can follow the disillusion point back into the luminous void that is centerless—the openness that is everything's ultimate identity, the great Who, the great What that is known as buddha nature. And if you cannot find anything to follow, just rest in that great silence, and be nothing for just one instant. Being nothing but pure awareness for an instant would be transformative in itself, and more than enough. Emaho!

When the mind starts to move, as it will, and thoughts and feelings and physical sensations again begin to proliferate, turn the mind upon itself again instead of looking outward at outer phenomena, projections, and perceptions. Turn the searchlight inward and mind the mind, becoming more keenly aware of awareness itself. Continue this laserlike questioning of who and what is experiencing, who is thinking, who is hearing, who, what, where, how; and then let go and release—drop everything: drop body and mind—and sense who or what is present between thoughts and when thought has ceased, even for a moment. If you discover that you really do not know who you are, then that is enough. That is what is true for you in this moment, and that is sufficient truth for now.

Through the practice of rushen, outer objects are revealed to be similar to mirages, and inner experiences are seen to be like dreams. Ultimate reality is revealed as nothing that can be seen, and our natural state is revealed to be free and blissful awareness, just as it is, along with everything else, just as it is. This is our true identity, our radiant buddha heart and mind, which cannot be found elsewhere, which is closer to you than your own breath, closer to you than your body, closer than your mind.

This ultimate reality is the ultimate refuge—don't miss it! Why look for the great elephant of awakening in the jungle of doctrines and theories when he is already at home peacefully settled in front of your own hearth? Emaho, wondrous, amazing, yes! Things are not what they seem to be, or are they otherwise, so we might as well burst out laughing. Ha!

7

TREKCHOD

⁕

Everything is found within the natural state,
so do not seek elsewhere.

—PADAMPA SANGYE

The central practice of the Dzogchen teachings is called *trekchod*. Trekchod means "seeing through," "cutting through," or "being through and through." The practice of trekchod is a means of cutting through duality, seeing through outward empty luminous appearances and perceptions, inwardly seeing through empty luminous experiences and empty luminous mind, and finally seeing through the empty luminous experiencer. The process of trekchod is to realize the empty luminous groundless ground of being, the instantaneous presence of total naked awareness, or rigpa—the pure presence of transpersonal being, not merely your individual, personal being. Trekchod is the great meditation renowned as nonmeditation or beyond meditation, called "enlightenment without meditation."

It is said that world-weariness and nonattachment are the legs of meditation, trust and devotion are the head of meditation; and nondistraction and presence of mind are the heart and body of meditation. In the beginning of meditation, the mind seems like a roaring waterfall; later it becomes like a rushing river, which gradually quiets down. Ultimately it becomes calm and clear like a lake or like the peaceful ocean where all rivers join. Simply remain without disturbance in all three of these stages of meditation, recognizing them all as different states of the same flow of awareness.

Trekchod is a practice that needs to be experienced, not conceptualized. I will guide you through a session of trekchod on Track 4 of the enclosed CD. Remember that when practicing this form of natural meditation you should rest relaxed and aware and let the mind unfurl like the infinite sky. Trust the wisdom of being, of simply allowing—openness and awareness inseparable. Rest in the radiant, open, skylike nature of mind, relying on innate wakefulness and natural awareness while doing nothing more. Just *being*. Some have called this Big Mind meditation or Sky Mind meditation. Tibetans call it Sky Yoga (*namkha naljor*) or SkyGazing meditation.

Let the body rest like a mountain—firm, imperturbable, bearing everything. Let the breath and energy flow naturally, like the ocean's waves, and enjoy the great state of nonaction. This is the time to savor and appreciate letting go—which means letting come and go—and letting be. Trekchod or Sky Mind meditation can be practiced anywhere, in any posture, anytime, for whatever duration. As for sessions and time periods, many quickies are said to be more effective than few prolongies. Keep it vividly fresh.

Do not let ice form on the free flowing waters of innate awareness by sticking to old holding patterns or by resting quietly in temporarily pleasant states of mind such as nonthought, bliss, or clarity; break these up by looking into Who is peaceful, who is thought-free, who is blissful. And then suddenly drop everything and let go, release, breathe deeply, and start again—fresh, vividly present, wakeful.

Moment by moment, as things arise to consciousness—thoughts, feelings, perceptions, memories, physical sensations in the body—continuously practice the fourfold cutting through technique of trekchod. First: seeing/perceiving whatever momentarily presents itself, as if in the magic mirror of mind. Second: recognizing whatever comes up simply as reflections and displays of innate awareness. Third: penetrating whatever arrives with the intuition of emptiness and insubstantiality and unreality. Fourth: releasing into the openness and awareness of natural meditation, just being present and aware. This is called "seeing, recognizing, penetrating, releasing."

✳ LISTEN TO TRACK 4 *Trekchod: Seeing Thru*

PRACTICING TREKCHOD ON YOUR OWN

Once you have practiced along with the guided session of trekchod on the enclosed CD, you can practice Sky Mind meditation on your own. The essence of this practice is awareness that is aware of awareness—not me looking at something or meditating, or the subject–object interaction of our usual dualistic framework. This awareness that is aware of awareness is the nondual wholeness and completeness of the radiant totality of empty cognizance; functioning spontaneously, unimpeded, unhindered; recognizing everything as adornments of awareness rather than distractions or impediments; and enjoying the entire spectacle as it goes by. Not waiting for something to happen or hoping or expecting; not feeling or doubting whether anything will happen or what you can get out of it; without comparing, competing, hurrying, hesitating or hanging back; not collecting, gathering, or trying to remember your experiences; free from judging whatever arises as either good or bad, helpful or harmful; not reacting, interfering or trying to control; not dominating, demanding, grasping; never discouraged, never depressed, never despairing; neither excited nor elated; not pretending, showing off, or inauthentic in any way; not fabricating or contriving; not trying to construct anything, neither special states of mind nor bliss and special meditative experiences; not imagining, fantasizing, or visualizing; not projecting or overidealizing; not doubting, planning, or regretting; not letting go too soon; not letting go too late or becoming fixated; not looking for purity and rejecting impurity; not trying to conclude that there is one, none, or many.

It is far better to simply give up the multitude of proliferating thoughts and ideas, simply rest at home and at ease in the delectable, self-liberating natural Great Perfection: thus cracking the shell of ignorance, cutting through the net of confusion and illusion, demolishing duality, seeing through, being through and through, in the natural Great Perfection, in the natural mind free of fabrication, simply gazing nakedly into our intrinsic nature, free of adulteration by artifice, resting naturally in the innate Great Perfection.

It is said that where there are reference points, there will be a poisonous view. Where there are fixations and concepts, there is said to be a treacherous path of meditation. If there is adopting and rejecting, there is said to be faulty action; if there is a firm goal in mind, the true result will be hindered. So simply remain in the great state of nondistraction, free of clinging and grasping, in the natural meditation of the Great Perfection. Rest at ease in the infinite vast expanse of openness and awareness, the radiant totality, and do not strive endlessly.

Free of distraction and beyond clinging, attachment, and aversion; free of mind-made efforts and mental gymnastics; beyond intellect and concept; simply enjoy the luminous wakeful state of the radiant Great Perfection. Primordially pure since the beginningless beginning, spontaneously manifesting moment after moment, without discrimination, without conceptualization, remain uncontrived and enjoy the great equanimity, the great evenness and harmony of the radiant natural perfection. All the phenomena of nirvana are contained in the nature of mind. If there is one, it is perfect; if there are two, they are perfect; if there are many, they are each perfect in the natural buddha mind of the Great Perfection. Remaining in nonmeditation, you will accomplish naturally inherent buddhahood. In the nonexisting expanse of intrinsic awareness—rigpa—you will find the primordial buddha on your own seat in this very moment.

Once you have discovered this liberating point, rest at ease and at home in the radiant Great Perfection. Since your eyes are now open, do not abandon this panoramic awareness and expect to attain something elsewhere; do not leave the great elephant of awakening and search for its mere footprint in the dense jungle. Buddha himself said that the ultimate nature of intrinsic mind is perfectly pure, profound, quiescent, uncompounded and unconditioned, unborn and undying, luminous and free since the beginningless beginning. Take your buddha seat, in the citadel of primordial enlightenment. This is the fruit of the path of the Great Perfection.

8

SKYGAZING MEDITATION

❧

When I dissolve into that vast expanse—
empty and clear—without end, without limits—
There is no difference between mind and sky.

—LAMA SHABKAR

SkyGazing is the core practical application of Dzogchen meditation. It is how we learn to relax, let go, and let be in the natural
state of things, just as they are. It is my favorite form of trekchod
practice and natural meditation.

Through this practice of natural meditative awareness, our
innate wakefulness completely unfurls and reveals itself. We
gradually release our small, narrow, egotistical, dualistic minds
into the nondual, skylike, infinite buddha mind, while meditating on the expansive, inclusive nature of rigpa: our natural
wisdom-mind and innate wakefulness. In this practice, we merge
the finite, thinking heart-mind with the absolute, unconditional
infinity of essential buddha-like being.

The sky—which represents the element of expansive space in this meditation practice—is without shape or color. No one can say exactly where it begins or where it ends. It just is. This makes it an ideal subject or metaphor for Dzogchen meditation. SkyGazing meditation leads us into a way of being that is in perfect harmony, attunement, and oneness with nature, including everything and everyone around us—and with our own true nature, too. In SkyGazing meditation, we dissolve into the infinite by becoming one with the open sky.

There are three stages to SkyGazing meditation:

- Arriving
- Intensifying
- Allowing

ARRIVING

Sit on the floor, on a cushion, or in a chair. Your back should be erect, but not rigid. Rest your arms on your thighs, wherever they naturally fall. Your eyes remain open for this meditation.

INTENSIFYING

Bring your awareness to the out-breath. Do not change the rhythm or depth of your breathing—just notice how the air feels as it leaves your body. Your out-breath takes you outside of your small self and connects you with everything that is. Let the in-breath occur naturally, but without placing any special attention on it. Rest your gaze softly on your surroundings. About half of your attention should be on your breath, while the other half is aware of the sky.

ALLOWING

Lean back slightly and raise your gaze until the sky fills your field of vision. Open your senses to the elements. As thoughts, feelings, and perceptions arise—as they inevitably will—release them gently, without judgment. Neither follow nor suppress them. Just be a flow of pure energy in the infinite vastness of space.

It is important to keep in mind that there is no way to do this meditation "wrong." Whatever you feel, whatever you are aware of, is simply what is. Your practice is to keep letting go of the speedy, judgmental, reactive everyday mind and return to this restful, innate awareness. If you find your mind wandering or your body tensing, stop and relax. Take a break, take a deep breath, chant "AH," and start again—refreshed, vivid, wakeful. How long you manage to remain aware is not important: it is the quality of awareness not the quantity that counts. There need not be a struggle involved. You can start again every moment, every second. What is important is the quality of your experience. It might take a while to get used to this, but try to relax into it and let go of ordinary ideas about meditation and habitual reference points.

There is a guided session of SkyGazing meditation included as Track 5 on the enclosed CD. After you have learned the basic practice, I encourage you to practice on your own, gradually extending the periods of silent awareness, yet without forcing anything. Let the buddha within—your internal buddha nature—be your guide.

✳ LISTEN TO TRACK 5 *SkyGazing Meditation*

INFORMAL SKYGAZING

SkyGazing means opening up and decontracting, space-mingling, dissolving in the infinite. You can practice it at any time: while resting at home, taking a break at work, or during transitions in your day. At these times, simply gaze into the sky or any undifferentiated expanse of space—such as a ceiling (if you are lying in bed), a blank wall, or a green lawn. Use this infinite panorama of emptiness as a metaphor for openness and awareness, release your fixations and preoccupations, breathe out—and simply let go into it.

PRACTICING SKYGAZING ON YOUR OWN

SkyGazing meditation can be done indoors or outdoors. You begin by taking your meditation seat. Close your eyes, rest your hands wherever comfortable, take a deep breath, and then let it out. Then take another breath and relax. Let go. Drop everything, settle naturally, and rest at ease. Let any thoughts, emotions, or physical sensations pass by like waves in the sea or like clouds in the sky, while simply observing their transparent, rainbow like nature. Be still and rest in the present moment, in nowness. When you find your thoughts drifting off, gently return to open awareness. For just this moment, relax into a feeling that there is nothing to do right now, nothing to figure out, understand, or achieve. Simply be present, attentive, aware.

Breathe in and out, deeply and slowly, letting go a little bit more with each out-breath. Let everything quiet down naturally, by itself. Let the body settle naturally in its own place, in its own time. Let the mind also settle naturally, in its own way, in its own time. Let everything go; let be. The three essential components of this first part of the SkyGazing meditation are to breathe, smile, and relax.

When you have settled down and feel a sense of alertness, calmness, and present awareness, open your eyes and raise your gaze to the sky. Gaze evenly into space with a soft focus. Do not force a stare; just rest your eyes on and in the vast and undifferentiated spacious expanse before you. Space, like mind, has no beginning or end, no inside or outside, no actual form, no color, no size, no shape. Mingle your gaze with this space; merge yourself and your mind with infinite, empty space. Dissolve into space until you become spacious awareness itself. As you exhale, exhale into space, following your out-breath into external space. Allow all of your thoughts, feelings, sensations, and emotions to come and go freely, letting everything that enters your awareness dissolve into vast space, and experience the radiant transparency of free-flowing present awareness.

Continue gazing freely into vast space, into the open sky, with the crystal clarity of naked awareness, and let everything go. Breathe the sky in and out, and breathe and dissolve into the sky with your out-breath. Follow the out-breath all the way out into space. Mingle with the sky, and slowly dissolve totally into the spacious joy of meditation. When a thought arises, watch it come, and watch it go. When a feeling presents itself, watch as it passes away by itself, without interference or manipulation. When you become aware that the quality of your attention is fading, see if you can bring it back by returning your attention to the natural in-and-out motion of the breath, focusing your attention on following your out-breath and letting everything dissolve with it. Continue this process until you are resting evenly in luminous centerless emptiness.

9

CHANTING THE HUNG MANTRA

Through the internal way of profound
HUNG recitation,
Clinging to appearances is stopped and
the power of awareness increases.

—GURU PADMASAMBHAVA

Chanting is a form of sacred music—of sublime enchantment—and an important part of spiritual practice in many different traditions the world over. Sacred chant and ritual music can help put us in better contact with and connect us to that which is greater than ourselves. Chant is one of humankind's most ancient, timeless, and universal therapies, effective on many levels. In the Himalayas, mantras (sacred words of power) and chants are constantly on the lips of people of all ages, from children to the oldest of the elders. We have already experienced chanting the "AH" mantra as part of the morning wake-up SkyBreath practice in Chapter Six. The Dalai Lama's mantra and the most popular mantra in Tibet is "OM MANI PADME HUNG" ("the jewel is in the lotus"): the mantra of love and compassion.

Chanting utilizes sacred sound as a transformational device. It is also a mind/body contemplative practice that opens and stimulates both sides of the brain. It can open up the mind and heart, untie knots in our subtle energy channels (opening our chakras in the process), and free us from all kinds of neuroses, hang-ups, and illnesses. In Tibetan chanting, we also add breath awareness and visualizations to our vocalization of the mantra to create a complete Vajrayana practice that can awaken and liberate us through the three pure-energy dimensions of body, speech, and mind. This practice aligns the outer, inner, and secret mystical levels into one all-encompassing awareness, which masterfully includes and integrates all the various dimensions or sheaths of our being.

There are numerous kinds of mantras of different lengths, for different purposes, visualized in different colors, and activating various chakras (subtle energy centers) throughout our inner body. These include one-syllable mantras like the cosmic sound of "OM"; the easily memorized Dzogchen mantra that we have already practiced, "AH"; three-syllable mantras like "OM AH HUNG"; hundred-syllable purification mantras; healing mantras; wisdom mantras; compassion and loving-kindness mantras; mantras for focusing energy; peacemaking and harmonizing mantras; magnetizing mantras; obstacle-removing mantras; secret mantras; and so on.

Particularly useful to this daily practice program is the Tibetan "HUNG" mantra, which is the seed syllable of wisdom and embodies the five wisdoms. In fact, the five parts of this Tibetan letter, pronounced "hoong," represent the five wisdoms: spacious-clarity wisdom, mirror like wisdom, discriminating wisdom, all-equalizing wisdom, and all-accomplishing wisdom (see

Figure 2). These five wisdoms are known in Tibetan Buddhism as our innate wisdom and as the inherent wisdoms that we can develop through this kind of practice so that we may apply them in the world for the benefit of all. There are masters, such as the Mahasiddha Humkara of ancient India, who made chanting this powerful, short mantra their entire practice.

There is a guided practice using the "HUNG" mantra included as Track 6 on the enclosed CD. Chanting can be a lot of fun. Enjoy HUNGing out with me.

✳ LISTEN TO TRACK 6 *HUNG Mantra*

CHANTING THE "HUNG" MANTRA ON YOUR OWN
Place your palms together in front of your heart, as though praying or supplicating. Buddhism is a nontheistic tradition; there is no one to whom you are actually praying. Rather, the gesture is intended to convey respect for everything that is, including your own buddha nature. According to the law of karma (cause and effect), and because all things are interconnected, every act of body, speech, and mind has a result. "For every action there is a reaction." Thus, prayer and affirmation are viewed as ways of making things happen.

You can chant the "HUNG" mantra at different times of the day or as part of your daily meditation practice. If you perform this mantra practice internally, rather than repeating the mantra out loud, the repetition should ride on your out-breath, as it would if you were to repeat it out loud. Sometimes try doing it five "HUNG"s at a time, with one big out-breath.

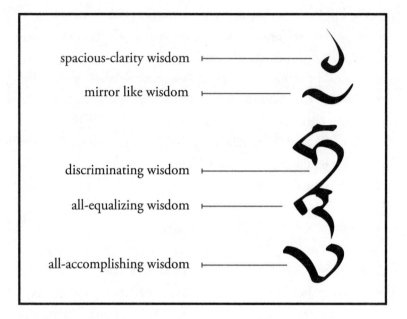

spacious-clarity wisdom ⊢——————

mirror like wisdom ⊢——————

discriminating wisdom ⊢——————

all-equalizing wisdom ⊢——————

all-accomplishing wisdom ⊢——————

Figure 2: The "five wisdoms" as represented in
the seed syllable HUNG in Tibetan

10

TOGAL

꒰ꙮ꒱

Luminosity is the nature of one's mind,
that eons of confusion cannot darken.

—LAMA SHABKAR

I t is often said that togal meditation is the best way to develop
stability in the trekchod view (the nature of mind) that we have
been introduced to and experienced through rushen and trekchod
practice. Togal is known as the utmost secret practice of Dzogchen,
and it means "being there" or "leap over." This is another practice
that can only be experienced, not conceptualized; I will present
the practice on the enclosed CD rather than attempting to explain
it fully here.

In togal, we endeavor to give rise to subtle visions or medita-
tional experiences, through which the trekchod practice of cutting
through becomes that much stronger, sharper, and deeper. In togal,
we come to perceive directly the clear light nature of the mind and

its manifestations as energy and forms, including all internal and external empty, radiant phenomena.

Togal is a visionary practice, the ultimate view being applied, actualized, and put into action. Ultimately, it results in the rainbow-light body of perfect enlightenment radiating in all directions, in all times and places at once, unborn and undying. Many Dzogchen masters ancient and modern have been known to have disappeared into rainbow light at the time of death, leaving no mortal remains behind, or in some cases leaving only hair and fingernails behind as signs of having accomplished the rainbow-light body.

Togal practice requires some effort and perseverance. When studied with a teacher, togal includes different postures and gazes, and requires going further into the practice beyond what is taught here, as well as making an effort toward increasing its duration. The version of togal taught in this program is best experienced by listening to Track 7 of the enclosed CD.

✳ LISTEN TO TRACK 7 *Togal: Being There*

DEDICATING THE MERIT

By doing these or any other spiritual practices, we accumulate merit—that is, we gather good karma and good fortune, we clear old karma, and we take a further step along the path of higher spiritual aspiration. Buddhist tradition recognizes the danger of becoming prideful and selfishly hoarding such merit for ourselves. This is why all Tibetan Buddhist practices end with a formal "dedication of merit": a declaration of our willingness to give away any merit we may have earned, with the intention that it may benefit all sentient beings and help us all achieve liberation and enlightenment.

You can dedicate the merit in whatever way holds personal meaning for you by saying and praying out loud, "I dedicate any merit I have accumulated by doing these practices to the benefit of all sentient beings"; by visualizing your compassionate aspiration embracing every living thing; by beaming light to them from your heart center or from your entire luminous being; or by any other way that helps you feel that you are truly giving away and sharing with others whatever inner peace, insight, and blessings you may have derived from your practice. To dedicate the merit and share the blessings is to acknowledge the profound interconnectedness of all things and to realize that none of us are truly free until all of us are free.

My own prayer goes like this:

May all beings everywhere
With whom we are inseparably connected
Be awakened, liberated, healed, fulfilled, and free;
May there be peace in this world, and an end to war,
violence, injustice, and poverty;
And may we all together complete the spiritual journey.

11

CREATING A MEDITATION PRACTICE

꠆

Just as a small child
Gradually develops its body and strength,
Dharma is in that same way,
From the steps of entering in the beginning
Up until the complete perfection.

—THE BUDDHA

M editation is a practice path—an experiment that we can undertake and experience for ourselves, something that can change and transform not only ourselves but all of our relationships, our entire life, and the world itself. Continuity is the secret of success. Just as the Grand Canyon was not formed in one day or one year, it takes time for the current of spiritual practice to cut deeply through all the ingrained habits and delusions we have built up over lifetimes. Regular spiritual practice erodes our fixations and selfishness. Over time, through continuing to practice, we learn from our own experience; this helps us to wise up, to open our hearts and minds, and to loosen prejudice and self-centered grasping, which changes everything, at least for us and those around us. Meditative mindfulness, like any genuine conscious inner work, can and does transform things, and on many levels.

Ideally, one should practice natural meditation every day. Many people find it helpful to practice spiritual disciplines like meditation at the same place and time each day, since a routine weaves it into your schedule more effortlessly. With regular practice, you will begin feeling more clarity, focus, and spaciousness in your life—and less of the tension, anxiety, and egoic claustrophobia that tends to make one irritable and unkind. I have found that spiritual practice is perfect. We just do it.

I advise you to enter into a daily meditation practice for whatever amount of time you have. Although an hour or a half hour is traditional, meditation practice is not about the quantity of time you invest in it but about the quality of awareness and intention brought to it. What is most important is a sincere passion and curiosity, an interest in truth and truth-seeking, in getting to the bottom of things. We all wish to develop our integrity and character and become more authentic. Meditative awareness helps us to realize who we truly are and are meant to be, why we are here, and brings us the clarity to see what can be done in this world, as well as how to do it. Your meditation practice is the path of your true vocation—which can lead to right livelihood, right action, and so forth, until you can eventually fulfill the goal of the Buddhist path and live the enlightened life. It is not as far away as you may think.

A Tibetan story tells us that the arrow-maker Saraha of India sang his pith instructions, called "The Royal Song of Saraha." He sang, "Straighten out your mind through meditation, like a fletcher straightens out his arrow, and hit the target every time." He said that those who do not drink their fill from the cool and soothing nectar of their masters' pith instructions will only be tortured by thirst and hunger on the endless desert plain of countless scholarly treatises.

Perhaps the ultimate pith instruction on the importance of meditation practice in the Tibetan lineage comes from the great meditator Milarepa, when his disciple, Gampopa, was going away into retreat after many years of studying. Milarepa had himself spent twenty years practicing Tantric yoga and meditation in a cave above the snow line, where he became as enlightened as the Buddha himself. Gampopa wanted to emulate his teacher and go into long retreat; he had already bowed three times, made offerings and said his good-byes to Milarepa, and had crossed a small stream and was walking away when Milarepa suddenly shouted out to him, "Hey, Gampopa!" And when Gampopa turned around, the saint Milarepa lifted his white cloth robe and showed him his bare buttocks, pock-marked and callused from years of sitting on a stone cave floor, as hardened as a horse's hoof. And Milarepa shouted, "Just do it!" Just wear out your butt through daily sitting meditation. As the Indian yogic saying goes, "Far better to wear out one meditation mat than to wear out hundreds of pairs of mendicants' sandals." Practice is perfect. Just do it.

MEDITATION IN ACTION

No matter how much you practice formal meditation and chanting, the true measure of your growth as a Dzogchen practitioner occurs in your daily encounters with the world. You will derive the greatest benefits from natural meditation if you see it as a continuous practice, extending beyond the time you spend in formal meditation. When you find yourself confronted with difficult situations, bring to mind the memory and sensation of vastness and spacious clarity that is available to you in your SkyGazing practice. Realize that this infinite universe is your natural habitat and that you are part of it and it is you. When you cannot sense this, there are merely some clouds obscuring the sky like nature of buddha mind. Natural meditation clears away the clouds so that you can see the reality of your own inherent freedom and innate perfection. Once you have experienced this glimpse of infinity, you can always remind yourself that the sky—the infinite, the timeless—is constantly and endlessly available to you, whatever the weather.

One of the most important instructions for us today is to remember that it takes two to tangle. It was in this sense that the great meditator Tilopa gave Naropa one of the most famous pith instructions: "It is not outer things that entangle us, Naropa; it is inner clinging and fixation that entangles us." Our experiences are like Velcro—they often have hooks attempting to hook us into the world, but, if we do not provide the rings, they cannot hook onto us.

That is why since time immemorial a secret of self-mastery and spiritual autonomy has been that it is not what happens to us, but what we make of it. that makes all the difference. It is not the causes and conditions and circumstances that occur in our lives that really determine our karma, our character, our experience, or our destiny. It is what we make of those experiences that determine our karma, our character, our experience, and our destiny. The winds of karma—that is, the winds of conditioning, individual and collective, local and global—may blow from the past, yes. But we can learn how to use the tiller better, how to better set the sails, how to sail better, how to use the wind or the force of the opponent so that rather than letting it blow us away, we can even learn to tack into the wind to get to where we choose to go. Let us never forget that we are the tiller of our own boat, and the steering wheel of our great vehicle is in our own hands.

As the Buddha himself said, "Who can make me angry if there are no seeds of anger in my heart-mind?" It is not others who make us angry; it is the seed of anger that exists within us, and others just provide a contributing cause. But, just like the weather cannot grow crops if there are no seeds in the ground, if we root out the seeds of the virulent, conflicting emotions within our hearts and minds, no one else can bring them out of us. Likewise, we should not think that others, outer circumstances, or conditions can really make us happy or give us any answers that we do not first experience as true in ourselves.

Padmasambhava—from whom these teachings in Tibet descend—gave one of the most famous pith instructions regarding the view of meditation in action. He said, "Though my view is higher than the sky, my actions regarding cause and effect are as meticulous as finely ground barley flour." In other words, though his view was higher than the sky and included the great emptiness, the vast void, the mystery of things in which everything is ultimately nothing in the complete analysis of the vast sweep of geologic time and space; even with such a vast view of *mahashunyata*—the luminous infinite void—still his actions and his conduct regarding cause and effect and interconnectedness remained meticulous, like finely ground flour, because every little thing counts, and for every action there is a reaction. The seed of our future lies in our every movement, our every thought, and our every word, once we understand the truth of how every deed creates a reaction and has karmic implications.

In the ultimate analysis, it may be that someday all living things will be gone, and even the planet Earth will eventually be dissolved into the sun in a fiery conflagration. But that probably will not be the final cycle of cosmological history. Even though it may be true that everything human will someday be obliterated, that does not matter in the here and now. What does matter is how we treat our family, our friends, our colleagues, and our children. Do we hug our children and smile at them, or do we abuse them, growl, and ignore them? In the pure and pristine present moment, it is clear that this is what is most important, and it would be insane to think otherwise. Spiritual wisdom, if nothing else, must be rooted in the highest and most elemental form of sanity.

SPIRITUAL REBIRTH

It is helpful to remember that, from a Buddhist point of view, you are capable of changing old habits at any moment—no matter how long you have been stuck in painful, unproductive patterns of living. Science tells us that almost every cell in your body changes every seven years. You do not have the same body you had ten or twelve years ago; none of us do. In this sense, you are not exactly the same person you were yesterday; none of us are. What happened to the person you were a month ago, a year ago, or ten years ago?

If you are not comfortable with the traditional Buddhist concept of rebirth, consider it this way: in this life, you are reborn every moment, with each renewed breath. Every single second is a rebirth, a time when you recreate yourself and your self-concepts.

Every day you wake up, it is exactly the same day—a brand new day, like the dawn of creation—but you can recreate it, according to your interpretations, or you can continue to relive the same daily dramas. Can you change? Where will you go? What will you do? Will it be different?

We are all drawn to the familiar when something or someone resonates familiarity. Your conditioning responds with what modern psychologists call a return to the patterns of your family of origin. However, you can break the pattern; you can change the next moment. We must change our lives—and for the better. You can do something different, something enlightened, creative, imaginative, and fresh, something compassionate and wise. That is a rebirth that you can accomplish in the immediate here and now.

Milarepa practiced alone and became enlightened in desolate Himalayan caves; his devotion and diligence were so great that he has continued to serve as an inspiration for generations of spiritual practitioners, sparking an entire practicing lineage of Tibetan yogic masters that continues today. Yet in his youth, Milarepa was a vengeful sorcerer, responsible for several deaths. Fearful for his karmic future, Milarepa became determined to change his evil karma—and he succeeded. In the "One Hundred Thousand Songs of Milarepa," he sang:

The fear of death and infernal rebirth due to my evil actions
has led me to practice in solitude in the snowcapped mountains.
On the uncertainty of life's duration and the
moment of death I have deeply meditated.
Thus I have reached the deathless, unshakeable

citadel of realization of the absolute essence.
My fear and doubts have vanished like mist
into the distance, never to disturb me again.
I will die content and free from regrets.
This is the fruit of Dharma practice.

Milarepa was spiritually reborn on those Himalayan peaks, and, in the process, he entirely purified and transformed himself and his karma and reached perfect enlightenment in a single lifetime. This is what is known as spiritual rebirth. This is the hope and promise of all authentic spiritual practice, and it is available to each of us, no matter what our past or present situation is.

May you know your innate buddha nature in this lifetime, so that all sentient beings may benefit from your passage through this world. May your natural meditation practice bring peace to you and all those around you.

AFTERWORD
Tibet, The Land of Snows

The Himalayas with their high snow peaks are dancing,
Joining my rhythm in the dance, Joining with the stillness,
The most dignified movement of them all.

—CHOGYAM TRUNGPA RINPOCHE

Tibet, the land of snows, is one of the last, great, extant wisdom cultures to have survived intact from ancient times. Tibetan Buddhist culture is a gold mine of the complete, living Buddhist teachings: a vast repository of timeless wisdom and compassionate skillful means conducive to a saner, healthier, more loving life and a safer, better world.

These teachings remained preserved in the Buddhist culture of Tibet, virtually unchanged, from the seventh century until the 1950s, when Chinese Communists conquered the country. The invaders killed 1,200,000 Tibetans, razed 6,000 monasteries, and suppressed both Tibet's native culture and its Buddhist religion. One hundred thousand Tibetans, including the Dalai Lama, fled to India and the surrounding countries. The practice of Buddhism was entirely suppressed.

Tibet's new inhabitants soon outnumbered its native citizens, making Tibetans a minority in their homeland. Schoolchildren go to Chinese schools and are taught to reject the old ways of their forebears and Buddhist traditional culture. Refugees still escaping into India and Nepal report continuing attempts to reduce the Tibetan culture and population through forced sterilization, forced abortions, and intermarriage. Since the Chinese takeover, 50 percent of the country has been deforested, and Tibet is now used for nuclear testing and the disposal of nuclear waste. Many Tibetan Buddhist monks and nuns have been jailed and defrocked for their nonviolent protests against these and other violations of the land and its people. Tibetan language and culture are on the verge of extinction.

Tenzin Gyatso—the Fourteenth Dalai Lama—was among those forced into exile in 1959. As both Grand Lama and the leader of the Tibetan government in exile, he is today both the spiritual and temporal leader of his country. In 1989, he was awarded the Nobel Peace Prize for his efforts to free Tibet through nonviolent means, as well as for his human rights advocacy and peacemaking around the world. The Dalai Lama now lives in Dharamsala, India. He continues to travel and teach extensively on the values of compassion and forgiveness, as well as on the ethics, philosophy, and practice of Buddhism.

In an effort to preserve Tibet's important cultural and spiritual heritage, a portion of the proceeds from this book will be donated to the Tibetan Buddhist Resource Center in New York City, E. Gene Smith's ambitious project to preserve all extant Tibetan texts and literature. For more information, you can contact them at:

The Tibetan Buddhist Resource Center
at the Rubin Museum of Art
150 W. 17th Street
New York, NY 10011
212-620-5000
www.tbrc.org

ADDENDUM: PITH INSTRUCTIONS

❦

The pith instructions included here and throughout this book are some favorites from my personal collection. May these be of use in helping you to awaken. Emaho!

The seeker who sets out upon the way shines bright over the world.
—GAUTAMA BUDDHA

Dzogchen is how things actually are.
—NYOSHUL KHENPO RINPOCHE

Seeing the Buddha-face of the self-mind is supreme:
How can common meditation match it?
—MILAREPA

One is introduced directly to one's own nature.
—GARAB DORJE, THE LAUGHING DIAMOND MASTER

A moment's realization of the luminosity of one's mind
Purifies the accumulated evil deeds and obscurations of countless eons.
—LAMA SHABKAR

The arising of realization is like the dispelling of darkness by the sun.
—LONGCHEN RABJAM

He in whose heart the words of the master have entered
Sees the truth like a treasure in his own palm.
—SARAHA

Though the nature of awareness is present in everyone
It depends on the dharmakaya pith instruction.
—THE GREAT SECRECY, THE TANTRA OF NO LETTERS

Swoop down from above with the absolute view [shunyata]
While climbing up the spiritual mountain from below
Through relative practices according to your capacity.
—GURU RINPOCHE PADMASAMBHAVA

Having dispelled the heart's darkness—
great ignorance—in its own place
The undiminished sun of luminous clarity shines continuously.
This good fortune is the kindness of the Lama, the only father.
Unrepayable kindness! Only remember the Lama!

—DUDJOM RINPOCHE

True blessings are the oral instructions on how to become enlightened
in a single lifetime, which you can receive from a qualified master.

—TULKU URGYEN RINPOCHE

Leave everything as it is in fundamental simplicity,
and clarity will arise by itself.
Only by doing nothing will you do all there is to be done.

—DILGO KHYENTSE RINPOCHE

AH is the supreme syllable,
The sacred syllable of all meaning.
Arising from within, it is without arising.
Beyond verbal expression,
It is the supreme cause of all expressions.

—THE MAGICAL NET OF MANJUSHRI

Unless samsara and nirvana are separated,
Your body, speech, and mind's ties
To the three realms [of conditioned existence] will not be cut.
Therefore, separate samsara and nirvana.

—DRA TALGYUR ROOT TANTRA

Unless we clarify the difference between samsara and nirvana,
our body, speech, and mind will continue to spin through
the three realms of samsara, which is pointless.
—TULKU URGYEN RINPOCHE

Leave it as it is, and rest your weary mind.
—LONGCHENPA

Unobscured by clouds or darkness,
the sun shines in the sky by its very nature.
—LONGCHENPA

This is the practice where you push the primordial Buddha off his seat.
—DUDJOM RINPOCHE

Direct your eyes toward the expanse of sky.
—SHRI SINGHA'S INSTRUCTION TO PADMASAMBHAVA

Leave alone the present wakefulness like a totally clear sky.
—LAMA SHABKAR

Rest at ease in the infinite vast expanse, and don't rely
on the hardships of hundreds of paths.
—NYOSHUL KHENPO RINPOCHE

Gazing into space, my mind blended with the infinite expanse of sky.
—LAMA SHABKAR

To mix awareness and experience,
crack the eggshell of ignorance.
Cut the web of existence.
Open awareness like the sky.

—NYOSHUL KHENPO RINPOCHE

The nature of the mind is the ultimate sphere, like space.
The nature of space is the nature of the mind, the innate nature.
In meaning they are not separate.
They are the oneness of the Great Perfection.
Please realize the nature at this very moment.

—LONGCHENPA

The Body of the Dharma is in itself Peace,
And therefore it has never emerged from itself;
And yet Light is kindled in the womb,
And from the womb and within the womb the play of blessings arise;
That is to say, the energy of compassion begins its ceaseless operation.

—CHOGYAM TRUNGPA RINPOCHE

Beyond both action and inaction, the supreme Dharma is accomplished.
So simply preserve the natural state, and rest your weary mind.

—DZA PATRUL RINPOCHE

As far as the sky pervades, so does awareness.
As far as awareness extends, so does absolute space.
Sky, awareness, absolute space,
Indistinguishably intermixed:
Immense, infinitely vast—
The ground of samsara, ground of nirvana.
To remain day and night in this state—
To enter this state easily—this is joy.
Emaho!

—LAMA SHABKAR

Don't investigate the roots of things,
Investigate the root of Mind!
Once the mind's root has been found,
You'll know one thing, yet all is thereby freed
But if the root of Mind you fail to find,
You will know everything but nothing understand.

—GURU PADMASAMBHAVA

Knowing the one that frees all, sustain the natural face of self-awareness.

—DUDJOM RINPOCHE

May we gain conviction in the view
Wherein samsara and nirvana are the same.
May we have consummate skill in meditation,
a natural flow unaltered, uncontrived.
May we bring our action to perfection, a natural,
unintended spontaneity.
May we find the dharmakaya,
Beyond all gaining and rejection.

—H. H. DUDJOM RINPOCHE

Don't invite the future
Don't pursue the past
Let go of the present
Relax, right now.

—GAMPOPA

Let thoughts go free, just like a dove released from a ship
in the middle of the infinite ocean.
For just as the bird finds nowhere to land
but back on the ship, thoughts have no place to go
other than returning to their place of origin.

—MAITRIPA

Give up the mind that wants to meditate and calm down.
Focus on nothing at all.
Disturbing thoughts and lazy indifference are not liberation.
Remain unstained by thoughts and circumstances;
Rest relaxed in the uncontrived nature of mind,
free of elaborations or alteration.
For the benefit of one and all, simply preserve peerless awareness.

—SUKKHASIDDHI

Nothing whatsoever, yet everything is experienced!
Simply recognize this appearance-void as magical display of awareness.
Let it remain naturally.
Don't spoil it by tampering and worrying about being right or wrong.
The ultimate luminosity of Dharmakaya
[absolute reality/buddha mind] is this unfabricated, natural mind.

—JAMGON KONGTRUL RINPOCHE

Cultivate the awareness that abides nowhere.

—GAUTAMA BUDDHA

Crush the eggshell of the mind and unfold your wings in the open sky;
Destroy the hut of duality and inhabit the
expansive mansion of awareness;
Ignorance—dualistic thinking—is the
great demon obstructing your path.
Slay it right now and be free.

—NYOSHUL KHENPO RINPOCHE

In meditation, be free of clinging to experiences.
—PADAMPA SANGYE

*Don't go into the tangled jungle looking for
the great awakened elephant who is already resting
quietly at home in front of your own hearth.*
—LAMA GENDUN RINPOCHE

Don't contrive, don't contrive, don't alter your mind.
—NYOSHUL KHENPO RINPOCHE

*Dzogpa Chenpo is how things actually are. Things left just as they are.
The natural state. How things actually are, their true mode of being.
The great knowledge holder, lineage master Jigme Lingpa, the fearless
master who lived three hundred years ago in Tibet, said, "Teachings
about Dzogchen are many. Knowers of Dzogchen are few." [The] great
Khenpo Ngawang Palzang, disciple of Patrul Rinpoche, the great
Dzogchen master, said, "Dzogchen is extremely simple, but not easy."
It is easy for anybody to point to the sky. It is easy for anybody to say
something about Dzogchen and how everything is perfect in its true
nature. But most people see the finger and they don't see the sky. So
if you see the finger and you didn't see the sky, then there is ngondro,
refuge, bodhichitta practice, a lot of meditations and purifications to do
in order to purify and dispel the obscurations temporarily obscuring our
buddha nature, our own true nature.*
—FROM *NATURAL GREAT PERFECTION: DZOGCHEN TEACHINGS
AND VAJRA SONGS* BY NYOSHUL KHENPO AND LAMA SURYA DAS

GLOSSARY

Terms are in Sanskrit, unless otherwise noted.

AH: the mantra associated with the throat chakra and the primordial sound from which everything arises.

bodhi: to awaken.

bodhichitta: "awakened heart-mind"; the absolute mind of enlightenment; the altruistic aspiration for enlightenment.

buddha: "awakened one"; a person who has achieved the enlightenment that leads to release from the cycle of existence and has thereby attained complete liberation, ultimate happiness and fulfillment, wisdom, love, and compassion.

chakra: "wheel"; generally refers to the body's seven subtle energy centers.

Dharma: the cosmic law; truth; the "great norm" underlying our world; the teaching of the Buddha, who recognized and formulated this law; thus, the teaching that expresses the universal truth.

Dharmakaya: one of the three bodies, or dimensions, of Buddha's manifestation—in this case, the unmanifested or formless form.

doha: spontaneous song of realization.

Dzogchen: (Tibetan) "Great Perfection" or great completeness.

emaho: (Tibetan) "wondrous"; the shortest Dzogchen teaching.

karma: "action" or "reaction"; conditioning; the universal law of cause and effect—the mental, verbal, and physical actions that lead to further consequences.

Machig Labdron: (1055–1153), Tibetan female master and disciple of Indian guru Padampa Sangye, the source of the Chod (Ego-Cutting) lineage in Tibet.

maha ati: a Sanskrit term for Dzogchen, or the Great Perfection.

mahamudra: "great seal"; one of the highest teachings of Tibetan Buddhism; the realization of emptiness and freedom.

mani: "jewel," symbolizing compassion in the mantra of Avalokiteshvara, "OM MANI PADME HUM."

mantra: a power-laden syllable or series of sacred syllables that manifests certain cosmic forces and the deepest essence of things.

mar-tri: (Tibetan) "red guidance"; that is, the naked truth.

men-ngak: (Tibetan) pith instructions.

mudra: symbolic hand gesture, often used in rituals and found in religious iconography.

nirvana: total enlightenment; complete liberation from suffering and confusion; ultimate peace and bliss, implying the fullest actualization of all the highest qualities innate in us; the complete overcoming of desire, hatred, and delusion; the goal of spiritual practice in all branches of Buddhism.

phowa: (Tibetan) consciousness transference; a special technique that permits one to intentionally transfer one's consciousness to a pure buddha-paradise at the moment of death.

rigpa: (Tibetan) total awareness; innate wakefulness; pure presence.

rushen: (Tibetan) subtle discernment.

samadhi: meditative absorption.

samskara: karmic imprint.

satori: (Japanese) "break through"; term used for enlightenment experience in Japanese Zen.

seed mantra: one-syllable mantric utterance like "OM," "AH," "HUNG," thought to contain the essence of a deity or samadhi.

shunyata: luminous emptiness.

Tantra: a type of nondual Buddhist teaching that emphasizes esoteric practices, direct experience, and contemplative arts rather than philosophical concerns.

tonglen: (Tibetan) "giving and receiving"; a breathing meditation that exchanges self for others; part of the Mahayana attitude transformation tradition.

tripitaka: "three baskets"; the threefold collection of authoritative original texts of Buddhism comprising the early canon.

tukarpo: (Tibetan) universal panacea.

upadesha: pith instructions.

upaya: "skillful means"; helpful methods a teacher uses to guide students to liberation.

Vajrayana: "diamond path" or "indestructible vehicle"; the Tantric school of Buddhism predominant in Tibet.

vinaya: the vows and disciplines of Buddhist monastics.

yana: "vehicle"; one of the three to nine approaches to liberation espoused by different schools of Buddhism.

Yeshe Tsogyal: "Ocean of Primordial Wisdom"; a great Tibetan dakini, she was Padmasambhava's main disciple, consort, and partner in establishing Buddhism in Tibet.

yoga: "yoke"; originally used in Hinduism to express the harnessing of self to the divine; the fundamental unity experienced through spiritual practice (also used to refer to the practices themselves). Commonly used today for physical movement practices such as hatha yoga. In Tibetan, yoga (*naljor*) means "reunion with the natural state."

ADDITIONAL RESOURCES

Batchelor, Stephen. *Buddhism without Beliefs: A Contemporary Guide to Awakening.* New York: Riverhead Books, 1998.

Chödrön, Pema. *When Things Fall Apart: Heart Advice for Difficult Times.* Boston: Shambhala Publications, 2000.

———. *Freedom in Exile: The Autobiography of the Dalai Lama.* San Francisco: HarperSanFrancisco, 1991.

———. *Dzogchen: The Heart Essence of the Great Perfection.* Ithaca, NY: Snow Lion Publications, 2004.

Chokyi Nyima Rinpoche. *Indisputable Truth.* Hong Kong: Rangjung Yeshe Publications, 1996.

Dalai Lama, H. H. the. *The World of Tibetan Buddhism: An Overview of Its Philosophy and Practice.* Trans., ed., and annotated by Geshe Thupten Jinpa. Boston: Wisdom Publications, 1995.

Epstein, Mark, M.D. *Thoughts without a Thinker: Psychotherapy from a Buddhist Perspective.* New York: Basic Books, 1995.

Goldstein, Joseph. *Insight Meditation: The Practice of Freedom*. Boston: Shambhala Publications, 2003.

Kornfield, Jack. *A Path with Heart: A Guide through the Perils and Promises of a Spiritual Life*. New York: Bantam Books, 1993.

Namkhai Norbu, Chogyal. *Dzogchen: The Self-Perfected State*. Ed. Adriano Clemente, trans. John Shane. Ithaca, NY: Snow Lion Publications, 1996.

Nhat Hanh, Thich. *Peace Is Every Step: The Path of Mindfulness in Everyday Life*. Ed. Arnold Kotler. New York, NY: Bantam Books, 1991.

Nyoshul Khenpo Rinpoche and Lama Surya Das. *Natural Great Perfection*. Ithaca, NY: Snow Lion Publications, 1995.

Patrul Rinpoche. *The Heart Treasure of the Enlightened Ones*. Explained by Dilgo Khyentse Rinpoche, trans. Mattheiu Ricard. Boston: Shambhala Publications, 1993.

Salzberg, Sharon. *Lovingkindness: The Revolutionary Art of Happiness*. Boston: Shambhala Publications, 1997.

Schmidt, Marcia, et al. *Dzogchen Essentials: The Path That Clarifies Confusion*. Hong Kong: Rangjung Yeshe Publications, 2004.

Sogyal Rinpoche. *The Tibetan Book of Living and Dying*. San Francisco: HarperSanFrancisco, 1992.

Surya Das, Lama. *The Snow Lion's Turquoise Mane: Wisdom Tales from Tibet*. San Francisco: HarperSanFrancisco, 1992.

Trungpa, Chogyam Rinpoche. *Shambhala: The Sacred Path of the Warrior*. Ed. Carolyn Rose Gimian. Boston: Shambhala Publications, 1988.

Tsoknyi Rinpoche, et al. *Carefree Dignity*. Hong Kong: Rangjung Yeshe Publications, 2004.

Urgyen Rinpoche, Tulku. *Repeating the Words of the Buddha.* Hong Kong: Rangjung Yeshe Publications, 1992.

———. *As It Is, Volume I.* Hong Kong: Ranjung Yeshe Publications, 1999.

———. *As It Is, Volume II.* Hong Kong: Rangjung Yeshe Publications, 2000.

ABOUT THE AUTHOR

Lama Surya Das studied with the great spiritual masters in Asia for over thirty years. He twice completed the traditional three-year Vajrayana meditation retreat in his teacher's Tibetan monastery in southern France. A leading spokesperson for the emerging Western Buddhism, he is a Dzogchen lineage holder and the founder of the Dzogchen Center. A poet, translator, activist, and full-time spiritual teacher, Surya Das lectures and leads meditation retreats and workshops worldwide, brings Tibetan lamas to the West to teach, and regularly organizes the annual week-long Western Buddhist Teachers' Conference with the Dalai Lama. Surya also writes a regular online "Ask the Lama" column at www.beliefnet.com and has long been active in interfaith dialogue and charitable projects in developing countries. Lama Surya Das is the author of many books, including *Letting Go of the Person You Used to Be: Lessons on Change, Loss, and Spiritual Transformation*; *Awakening the Buddhist Heart: Integrating Love, Meaning, and Connection into Every Part of Your Life*; *The Snow Lion's Turquoise Mane: Wisdom Tales from Tibet*; *Natural Great Perfection* (with Nyoshul Khenpo Rinpoche); *Awakening the Buddha Within: Tibetan Wisdom for the Western World*; and *Awakening to the Sacred: Creating a Personal Spiritual Life*. He writes regularly for *Tricycle, Body and Soul, Tikkun,* and other magazines, and he is currently working on a book about the Buddhist *paramitas*, the ten transcendental virtues and enlightening practices of the selfless bodhisattva.

ABOUT SOUNDS TRUE

Sounds True was founded in 1985 with a clear vision: to disseminate spiritual wisdom. Located in Boulder, Colorado, Sounds True publishes teaching programs that are designed to educate, uplift, and inspire. We work with many of the leading spiritual teachers, thinkers, healers, and visionary artists of our time.

To receive a free catalog of tools and teachings for personal and spiritual transformation, please visit www.soundstrue.com, call toll-free 800-333-9185, or write to us at the address below.

SOUNDS TRUE
PO Box 8010 / Boulder CO 80306